The Parish Guide to the New Evangelization

D1319109

The Parish Guide to the New Evangelization

An Action Plan for Sharing the Faith

Fr. Robert J. Hater

Our Sunday Visitor Publishing Division
Our Sunday Visitor, Inc.
Huntington, Indiana 46750

Nihil Obstat
Msgr. Michael Heintz, Ph.D.
Censor Librorum

Imprimatur
✠ Kevin C. Rhoades
Bishop of Fort Wayne-South Bend
September 4, 2012

The *Nihil Obstat* and *Imprimatur* are official declarations that a
book is free from doctrinal or moral error. It is not implied that
those who have granted the *Nihil Obstat* and *Imprimatur* agree
with the contents, opinions, or statements expressed.

Every reasonable effort has been made to determine copyright holders of
excerpted materials and to secure permissions as needed. If any copyrighted
materials have been inadvertently used in this work without proper credit being
given in one form or another, please notify Our Sunday Visitor in writing
so that future printings of this work may be corrected accordingly.

Copyright © 2013 by Robert J. Hater. Published 2013.

18 17 16 15 14 13   2 3 4 5 6 7 8 9

All rights reserved. With the exception of short excerpts for critical reviews, no
part of this work may be reproduced or transmitted in any form or by any means
whatsoever without permission in writing from the publisher. Contact: Our
Sunday Visitor Publishing Division, Our Sunday Visitor, Inc., 200 Noll Plaza,
Huntington, IN 46750; 1-800-348-2440; bookpermissions@osv.com.

ISBN: 978-1-61278-642-1 (Inventory No. T1338)
eISBN: 978-1-61278-321-5
LCCN: 2013931516

Cover design: Rebecca J. Heaston
Cover art: Shutterstock
Interior design: Sherri L. Hoffman

PRINTED IN THE UNITED STATES OF AMERICA

—

The Good News of Jesus first came into my life through the faith, hard work, and the dedication of my parents, Stanley and Olivia Hater. As early as I can remember, the Christmas crib; the statues of Jesus, Mary, and Joseph; and the crucifix reminded me that life is more than having fun and making money. The environment of our home that my parents established told me that Jesus is God and that the Church is vital in my life. These memories remain to this day, as do the sacrifices of my parents that enabled me and my brother and sisters to attend Catholic schools including college.

The little family store where my dad labored so hard taught me the value of work, reminding me that Jesus was a worker and how we can find God in honest, human labor, whatever it is. My mother's choosing to remain in our home daily and be present to the family was one of the greatest blessings of my life. As I watched her every day, I learned my first lessons in Christian evangelization — I learned that it is rooted in being present and in love.

In memory of them, and in appreciation for their love and sacrifice, I dedicate this book to my parents, Stanley and Olivia Hater.

Table of Contents

Foreword *by Father Alfred McBride, O.Praem.*   9

Acknowledgments   11

Introduction   13

One: Why the New Evangelization?   15

Two: The Parish, the Kingdom, and the New Evangelization   31

Three: The Parish in Contemporary Culture:
The Challenge to the New Evangelization   49

Four: The New Evangelization and Ministry   61

Five: The New Evangelization and the Parish   73

Six: The New Evangelization and the Ministries of Word,
Worship, and Service   89

Seven: The New Evangelization, Family, and Workplace   103

Eight: The New Evangelization and Christian Spirituality   117

Nine: The New Evangelization and Conversion   127

Ten: The New Evangelization — Catholic Style   137

Eleven: The New Evangelization and Pastoral Life:
A Practical Process   147

Conclusion   159

Foreword

By Father Alfred McBride, O.Praem.

Ever since Pope Paul VI's apostolic exhortation *On Evangelization in the Modern World* and Blessed John Paul II's encyclical *The Mission of the Redeemer*, there has been a growing call to the whole Church to become an evangelizing community. Pope Benedict XVI recently presided over a world Synod of Bishops on this call from the Holy Spirit, to show us how to make the new evangelization a reality.

Father Robert Hater's extraordinary book, *The Parish Guide to the New Evangelization*, is a brilliant, compassionate, and practical way for our over eighteen thousand parishes in the United States to accept the call to the new evangelization. I recommend his book to all our pastors. Father Bob's heart is in touch with the pulse of today's parishes. He accompanies every aspect of evangelization in clear language, with personal stories, discussion questions, and numerous practical guides to get started.

I think pastors will be relieved to know that the author is not proposing new programs or structures to make this happen. Instead, he presents a vision in which pastors, staff members, and families can become evangelizers — based on Christ's teachings about the kingdom of heaven as found in Scripture, liturgy, service, and Church documents throughout the centuries of faith communities, from the days of the apostles to our contemporary ministries.

Father Bob holds up these ideals in such a way that the fire of faith born in the center of the parish radiates out to its members, who in turn influence their workplaces. I was especially interested in how prudently and creatively he draws lessons from today's evangelical churches. He also sympathizes with priests who run three or four parishes and could benefit from this new evangelization. I like the way he gives positive advice regarding young people who thirst for an ardent prayer life, a love for Scripture, and a genuine understanding of the Eucharist, within our parish life, so as not to drift to evangelical churches.

The author practices the role of storytelling that he commends to evangelizing priests for their homilies. Rarely do many pages go by without personal stories that ratify his message. He often draws attention to the value of the social media. Several times he cites Brandon Vogt's perceptive guidance to Catholic blogs in his book *The Church and New Media* (Our Sunday Visitor, 2011), showing how Facebook, Twitter, i-Pods, i-Phones, etc., can be useful for evangelizing.

Father Bob also explains how the new evangelization can be useful in solving parish problems arising from partisan politics, infighting, and turf building. He proposes numerous solutions for transforming parishes into living communities. He writes that parish staff members can function better if they are "people persons." He has an interesting proposal for using a revolving leadership model for parish staffs that would change every two or three years, which would eventually roll back to where they started. His method of personalizing the life of the parish — with a spirit of welcoming, reconciling, and prayer, based on word, worship, and service — makes new evangelization accessible, attractive, and rewarding.

I had the privilege of spending time with Father Hater when he joined our group of priests for several summer weeks in Cape Cod. I see his personal qualities, so evident there, wonderfully present in his excellent book on evangelization.

Acknowledgments

I thank Bert Ghezzi for his invaluable help as I wrote this book on the new evangelization, a significant revision of *Catholic Evangelization: The Heart of Ministry*. He offered many suggestions in the development of *A Parish Guide to the New Evangelization*.

I am also grateful to the Office of Evangelization and Catechesis of the Archdiocese of Cincinnati, whose staff read the manuscript. In addition, I am extremely thankful to my friends Julie St. Croix of the Office of Faith Formation, St. John the Evangelist Church, Frederick, Maryland; to Joseph White of Our Sunday Visitor; and to Barbara Romanello-Wichtman, diocesan director of Religious Education and Catechesis, Columbus, Ohio, for their careful reading of the text, wise advice, and insightful commentary on the book.

The Scripture citations used in this work are taken from:

- The *Catholic Edition of the New Revised Standard Version of the Bible* (NRSV), copyright © 1989 and 1993 by the Division of Christian Education of the National Council of the Churches of Christ in the United States of America. Used by permission. All rights reserved.
- *The Jerusalem Bible* (JB), copyright © 1966 by Darton, Longman & Todd, Ltd., and Doubleday & Company, Inc. All rights reserved.

English translation of the *Catechism of the Catholic Church* (CCC) for the United States of America copyright © 1994, United States Catholic Conference, Inc. — Libreria Editrice Vaticana. English translation of the *Catechism of the Catholic Church: Modifications from the Editio Typica* copyright © 1997, United States Catholic Conference, Inc. — Libreria Editrice Vaticana.

Excerpts from the *General Directory for Catechesis*, Congregation for the Clergy, copyright © 1997, United States Catholic Conference, Inc.

— Libreria Editrice Vaticana. Excerpts from papal statements and other Vatican documents are copyrighted, © 2013, Libreria Editrice Vaticana.

Excerpts from *Called and Gifted for the Third Millennium* (1995), *Thy Kingdom Come: A Manual for Diocesan Evangelization Staff* (1999), *Co-Workers in the Vineyard of the Lord* (2005), *Sharing Catholic Social Teaching: Challenges and Directions* (1997), *National Directory for Catechesis* (2005), *Our Hearts Were Burning Within Us: A Pastoral Plan for Adult Faith Formation in the United States* (1999), *A Family Perspective in Church and Society: A Manual for All Pastoral Leaders* (1998), and *Disciples Called to Witness: The New Evangelization* (2012) are copyrighted, United States Conference of Catholic Bishops (USCCB).

Introduction

Evangelization, put simply, is the Christian's call to share the *Good News* of God's love and forgiveness, made possible because of Jesus' dying and rising from the dead. He invites us to profess the faith that we received at Baptism. This invitation is an ongoing one that calls us to enter ever more deeply into the mystery of God's love. It grows within us whenever we respond to God's invitation through our actions. It is essential in our lifelong journey with God.

We share God's love in our family, society, workplace, and church. A parent's love, a neighbor's compassion, an employer's just business practices, an employee's work, a parish's welcome, and the witness of a good life are forms of evangelization. All proclaim God's loving presence. As the U.S. bishops said in *Co-Workers in the Vineyard of the Lord*, "The basic call is the same for all the followers of Christ, namely 'That all Christians in whatever state or walk of life are called to the fullness of Christian life and to the perfection of charity, and this holiness is conducive to a more humane way of living even in society here on earth.'"*

A Parish Guide to the New Evangelization clarifies the role of the new evangelization and encourages us to develop an evangelizing spirit. It can benefit anyone interested in Catholic life, pastoral practice, and teaching, but it is directed primarily to pastoral leaders and ministers. These include: priests, deacons, parish administrators, coordinators of Catholic evangelization, evangelization teams, directors of religious education or catechesis, school principals, teachers, renewal coordinators, and RCIA directors.

Each chapter offers suggestions for reflection and pastoral action. They invite the reader to glean practical insights from the stories, messages, and theological content of the chapter.

I hope this book helps pastoral leaders as they carry out Jesus' call to proclaim God's love in our time. May its spiritual and pastoral approach help them respond to contemporary challenges.

---

* Second Vatican Council, *Dogmatic Constitution on the Church* [*Lumen Gentium*] (LG), no. 40, in *Vatican Council II: Constitutions, Decrees, Declarations* (rev. trans. in inclusive language), edited by Austin Flannery (Northport, NY: Costello Publishing, 1996).

Chapter One

Why the New Evangelization?

To clarify the meaning of the new evangelization, section one begins by asking, "What Is Catholic Evangelization?" The next section considers "Why the New Evangelization?" The third section addresses "What Is the New Evangelization?" The fourth section offers pastoral reflections and suggestions for action steps.

Parish pastoral ministers must be on the same page with each other when addressing the issue of the new evangelization. To make sure that this happens, this book begins by clarifying the notion of evangelization before it considers the new evangelization. The latter presumes the former, for the *Good News* that evangelization proclaims doesn't change. It has been the same from the time Jesus taught it and sent the first apostles and disciples to proclaim it to all nations. It is the responsibility of parish leaders to do the same.

We begin with a story of two evangelizers, Jim and Sally.

Jim and Sally live in a small mid-western town. Now retired, they enjoy walking through shops, greeting old friends, and meeting new ones. One afternoon they saw a young woman walking alone. She was a newcomer. They welcomed her. The woman's name was Connie.

Soon Connie, Jim, and Sally sat in an ice cream parlor. Connie was sad, so Jim and Sally invited her to their home. After a nice dinner and personal conversation, Connie expressed gratitude, and she then told them she had to leave. For several years, they never heard from her.

On Holy Thursday, five years later, they received a package. Opening it, Sally found a small frayed teddy bear and a letter, which read:

Dear Sally and Jim,

It's been a long time since we met. Remember five years ago when you bought me ice cream, invited me to your home for dinner, and listened to me? I was depressed but never told you why. The evening before, I learned I was pregnant. Unmarried and 19, I panicked, ran away, got off the bus in your town, and thought of hurting myself. Your love, concern, and prayers changed my mind.

When I left, Jim said, "Trust God, and you will be okay." Those words, your kindness and God's help saved my life. Enclosed find a small teddy bear. It is frayed and worn. This was my baby Erica's first toy. I want you to have it, as a reminder that two people, little Erica and me, owe you our lives. We are now fine. I pray that I can do for others what you have done for us.

Love,
Connie

Were Sally and Jim evangelizers? The answer is yes if we understand the term in light of the contemporary Catholic understanding of evangelization.

1. What Is Catholic Evangelization?

Before the Second Vatican Council (1962-1965), the word "evangelization" was not commonly used by pastors or in Catholic pastoral practice. Rooted in the thrust of this council, Pope Paul VI's apostolic exhortation *On Evangelization in the Modern World* (EN) set new directions for our understanding of evangelization.

Pope Paul stresses Jesus' life and ministry as the chief content of evangelization. Consequently, to appreciate evangelization, we look to Jesus in the Christian Scriptures, which reveal Jesus' evangelizing activities. In *On Evangelization in the Modern World*, the pope lists these as: Jesus' incarnation, his miracles and teachings, the gathering of the disciples, the sending out of the apostles, his crucifixion and resurrection, and the permanence of his presence in the Christian community. These activities remind all parish ministers that evangelization is more than words. It requires the active witness of faith, hope, and charity.

Pope Paul's emphasis moved Catholic scholars to look more deeply into the term evangelization. The word comes from the Greek term *euangelizo*, which means to convey good news. This may be the good news of a party, an athletic victory, or a family celebration. The Septuagint, or Greek translation of the Hebrew Scriptures, used this term in 2 Samuel and Psalms, as well as in the Prophets and Historical books. For example, Psalm 40:9 refers to the Good News that God has brought salvation.

Jesus spoke Aramaic and probably used the word *sabar*, for what subsequently was translated as *euangelizo* in the Greek Christian Scriptures. St. Paul used *euangelizo* to refer to Jesus' mission, ministry, life, and preaching. He used it, also, to indicate the activity of Christians, when proclaiming Jesus' Good News to nonbelievers.

The early Church used many other words for sharing the Good News of salvation. St. John used the word *marturein*, meaning to give witness. *Keruxate*, meaning to proclaim, was used too. This multiple use indicated that for the early Church, sharing the faith was the important thing.

Early Christian writers — such as Clement of Rome, Justin Martyr, Irenaeus, and John Chrysostom — used *euangelizo*. When Latin became prominent in Western Christianity, this word was translated as *evangelizo*. Subsequently, St. Thomas Aquinas and others used it as well.

Through the Middle Ages, *evangelizo* was translated into Old English and gradually into Modern English. John Wycliffe, Francis Bacon, Thomas Hobbes, and other scholars and religious figures employed it. Gradually, the term took two forms in English, "evangelism" and "evangelization."

During the nineteenth century, the word "evangelism" was used by Protestant churches, but the Catholic community used no such term for sharing the Good News. This changed in 1956, when Cardinal Suenens, in *The Gospel to Every Creature*, linked evangelization to the entire Christian endeavor. The preface to this book was written by the future Pope Paul VI, who revolutionized the Catholic use of the term evangelization. Today, this term, not evangelism, is employed in Catholic ministry to refer to sharing the Good News of God's love. Although its focus differs from the past, evangelization is a new word to refer to an old reality — namely, the invitation for Catholics to share their faith.

Since *On Evangelization in the Modern World*, subsequent Church documents have clarified the new direction initiated by Pope Paul VI. Blessed John Paul II stressed that catechesis is an aspect of the evangelization process in *On Catechesis in Our Time* (CT).

In *On the Permanent Validity of the Church's Missionary Mandate* (RM), John Paul II connected evangelization with the Church's missionary mandate. The United States bishops applied the new directions to this country in *Go and Make Disciples: A Plan and Strategy for Catholic Evangelization in the United State*s and in *Thy Kingdom Come: A Manual for Diocesan Evangelization Staff.*

In *The Church in America*, John Paul II stressed the vital role that evangelization must play in the future vitality of Christianity in the Americas.

The *General Directory for Catechesis* (GDC), a document prepared by the Congregation for the Clergy in Rome, in 1997, offers guidelines for catechesis throughout the world. It solidified and focused the developing notions of evangelization since Vatican II. This document sees evangelization as the thread that weaves through all Church ministries and the lives of Christians.

Following the lead of Pope Paul VI and Blessed John Paul II, Pope Benedict XVI issued a series of proclamations, stressing the vital role of future worldwide evangelization. His commitment to new evangelization efforts was indicated by his calling of the XIII Ordinary General Assembly of the Synod of Bishops for a worldwide synod on the new evangelization in 2012. The theme of this conference was *proclaiming the Gospel of Jesus Christ.*

Some Catholics do not understand the meaning of Catholic evangelization. Many associate it with evangelicals, especially the preaching of televangelists. Because evangelization is not widely understood by Catholics, even among some pastoral ministers, it is important to clarify its meaning. This clarification sees evangelization as the energizing spirit of all Church ministries and the Christian's life in the family and world. The Catholic Church teaches that evangelization is the heart and soul of Christian life and ministry. It happens whenever a Christian shares, directly or indirectly, Jesus' Good News.

The preparatory document for the 1973 world Synod of Bishops on evangelization described evangelization as "the activity whereby the Church proclaims the gospel, so that the faith may be aroused, may unfold, and may grow." This connects with Pope Paul VI's statement in *On Evangelization in the Modern World*, "For the church, to evangelize means bringing the Good News into all strata of humanity, and through its influence, transforming humanity from within and making it new" (n. 18).

The *General Directory for Catechesis* emphasizes that evangelization happens through words and deeds. It is "at once testimony and proclamation, word and sacrament, teaching and task" (n. 39). This document continues, "Proclamation, witness, teaching, sacraments, love of neighbor: all of these aspects are the means by which the one Gospel is transmitted and they constitute the essential elements of evangelization itself" (n. 46).

Evangelization: A Description

Evangelization embraces all aspects of a Christian's life. Seen in this way, *evangelization is a process fostering ongoing conversion within the Christian community that seeks to initiate people ever more deeply into the mystery of God's love as it is manifested most fully in the dying and rising of Jesus.*

First: Evangelization is the invitation to accept the Good News of God's love. Evidence of God's love, which first comes from life itself and sets the stage for Jesus' revelation, can be referred to as *implicit evangelization*, which often became the focus after Vatican II. Examples include the beauty of creation, the love of a parent, the compassionate listening of a friend, and social concerns of a parish. Even if Jesus' name is not mentioned, evangelization happens in implicit ways, thus preparing for more explicit manifestations of Jesus' saving word. It is critical, however, that both implicit evangelization and explicit evangelization happen.

Explicit evangelization proclaims the role of Jesus, God, the kingdom, and the Church in God's plan of salvation and gives deeper insights into God, who is already present in implicit evangelization. This can happen formally in a parish, classroom, or study group, and informally at home, with friends, or in the workplace.

Second: Conversion happens between God and individuals within a Christian community. Conversion is always communitarian, for we learn our deepest values from others. Even when conversion occurs in solitary moments, it happens because we live in a family, communicate with friends, work with associates, and worship with other people who influence us. Implicit and explicit evangelization foster ongoing conversion.

Third: Evangelization seeks to initiate people ever more deeply into the mystery of God's love. This initiation requires explicit proclamation of the Gospel. Bill, a friend of mine, told me that after an accident he discovered how God was speaking to him through his sickness.

This happened over a number of months and began with the visit of his uncle Joe, a deeply religious Catholic relative, when Bill was in the hospital. On the first visit, Joe brought him a crucifix and explained how meditating on Jesus' suffering helped him through the long and painful suffering he endured as his father was dying. As they spoke, Bill asked Joe to pray with him and read the biblical account of Jesus' suffering and death. The two continued this practice, even after Bill returned home, but was still confined there for several more months.

Sometime after he recovered his health, I met Bill at a parish function. He told me his story and stressed that in his sickness "The crucifix gave me hope and a reason to go on." As Bill grew to appreciate how it connected with his suffering, the Scripture passage took on new meaning for him. Reading the story of Christ's passion, meditating on the crucifix, and celebrating the Eucharist evangelized him in ways that his uncle's concern alone never could have done.

Fourth: Evangelization reveals that God's love is manifested most fully in the death and resurrection of Jesus. During my friend's sickness, he learned how Jesus' death reflected God's love. Søren Kierkegaard describes this love, climaxed on the cross, as "the supreme paradox." A God dying for creatures makes no sense to reason but becomes a source of salvation through faith. Jesus being raised from the dead by the Father is the final testimony, affirming that no matter what conclusions we draw from suffering, disappointment, or frustration, Christian faith teaches that God's love transcends death and promises eventual happiness.

Evangelization: Lifelong Process

Evangelization is the heart of ongoing conversion, in which God's Word doesn't change, but our ability to hear it changes, depending on our age and circumstances. This understanding differs from the evangelical Christians who emphasize hearing God's Word and accepting Jesus Christ once and for all in a definitive moment of conversion and salvation.

The risen Lord evangelizes in an ongoing way through the entire parish. Pastoral ministers have to continually emphasize this truth to their parishioners. For the Church, evangelization means "first of all to bear witness, in a simple and direct way, to God revealed by Jesus Christ, in the Holy Spirit; to bear witness that in his Son God has loved the world — that in His Incarnate Word he has given being to all things and has called men to eternal life" (*On Evangelization in the Modern World* [EN], n. 26). Consequently, evangelization means that again and again people hear the Good News of God's forgiveness because we forgive; that people see Christian hope because they witness our hope; and that people celebrate divine friendship because we dare to be friends.

In the evangelization process, the living Lord is experienced in flesh and blood — in the joys and tears of everyday life, because Christians are bold enough to live as if God is our loving Father. Evangelical witness "will always contain as the foundation, center, and at the same time summit of its dynamism — a clear proclamation that, in Jesus Christ, the Son of God made man, who died and rose from the dead, salvation is offered to all men, as a gift of God's grace and mercy" (EN, n. 27).

Evangelization in a parish involves the kingdom in action, telling society that the Word of Jesus is alive. Every day, family members proclaim God's Word to one another through patience, sacrifice, and generosity. Workers and managers proclaim God's Word in the workplace by following Gospel values of justice and fairness. Churches support and assist members through preaching, teaching, liturgy, counseling, and generous giving to the marginalized.

Evangelization is the lifeblood of Christian life and parish ministry. As an ongoing activity of the parish community, it includes the initial proclamation of the Word, as well as the various pastoral ministries that nourish this initial proclamation. The *General Directory for Catechesis* describes three necessary moments in the process of evangelization. They are *missionary activity* to proclaim the Good News to those who do not believe and/or who are religiously indifferent, *initial catechesis* for those who accept the Gospel and who seek to deepen their process of initiation into the faith, and *pastoral activity* directed to strengthening the faith of the mature Christian faithful in the Church (n. 49).

Evangelization: Holistic Approach

Evangelization receives further specification in the ministries of word, worship, and service, which are the heart of parish life. Consequently, evangelization happens in catechesis and preaching, prayer and liturgy, and service. Evangelization is holistic, where the various ministries converge into a totality.

Before this holistic view of evangelization came into focus, a more restricted approach was popular in some Catholic quarters. It saw evangelization and pre-evangelization as operative before a person makes a faith commitment. This approach was used in the 1960s and 1970s, especially in catechetical and missionary work.

In this more restricted approach, pre-evangelization, which sets the stage for evangelization, includes welcome, kindness, charity, and social concern that prepare people to receive God's Word. Once the climate is set, evangelization helps people learn about Jesus and the Church. As evangelization proceeds, and people look toward a faith commitment, catechesis begins.

This threefold movement is hinted at in the *Rite of Christian Initiation of Adults* (RCIA). Here, pre-evangelization and evangelization are operative in the pre-catechumenal stage. When the person chooses to become a catechumen, catechesis starts. Hence, evangelization is seen in terms of the initial proclamation of the Gospel, which is directed toward conversion and is followed by catechesis. In this approach, people are evangelized before and catechized after they make an initial faith commitment.

This view of evangelization emphasizes the importance of a parish setting as a proper climate for proclaiming God's Word and acknowledging a person's level of readiness. It becomes problematic, however, if the parish dichotomizes evangelization and catechesis, which are not an either/or; namely, first evangelization, then catechesis. Rather, as the holistic approach says, catechesis is an aspect or moment in the evangelization process itself (*On Catechesis in Our Time*, n. 18). In saying this, we remember also that catechesis is ongoing and takes different forms as a person matures in faith.

In proclaiming the lived reality of Jesus' dying, rising, and sending of the Spirit, parish evangelization energizes parish efforts, reminding parish leaders of their mission to live God's kingdom. Christian life is rooted in the lifeblood and marrow of evangelization. Without it, individual or institutional efforts to proclaim God's Word, celebrate it, and serve others lack the dynamism promised by Jesus' Good News.

2. Why the New Evangelization?

Pastoral ministers in their efforts to further the Good News of Jesus recognize that the world, society, and culture need spiritual renewal. More and more, materialism, technology-gone-wild, amorality, and relativism negatively affect our lives. As they spread throughout the globe, secular desires and achievements challenge spiritual values. This is particularly true in the United States and Europe, although it extends across the world. With this in mind, Pope Benedict XVI said, "Our own time, then, must be increasingly marked by a new hearing of God's word and a new evangelization" (*The Word of the Lord*, n. 122).

While the achievements of technology and the growth of economic culture bring countless benefits to humankind, they often lead to negative consequences. In their aftermath, more people, once Christian, now claim no religious allegiance. We run into such people at parish festivals, business meetings, and family parties. Recent data indicate that Catholics are leaving the Church in large numbers.

Pastoral leaders know of Church defections and the growth of evangelical churches, often claiming that over 50 percent of their members were once Catholic. These leaders can become discouraged at such statistics, especially when traditional Catholic ways to share Jesus' Good News and catechize children and youth don't work well. Often, pastoral ministers develop solid, adult faith-formation programs, but the number of those attending them is relatively small compared to the general Catholic population.

Culture, Customs, and Needs

Recent popes recognized the cultural challenges facing the Church. Beginning with Pope Paul VI's *On Evangelization in the Modern World*, they emphasized the need to look for new ways to bring Jesus' message to our time and to help people uncover the God who is there. They stressed that his Good News is proclaimed in cultures with different values and customs, which must be taken into account when evangelizing or catechizing. For instance, Hispanic-speaking teenagers in Fort Worth, Texas, must be instructed in the faith using different customs and language than Cambodian teenagers in New York. The same applies to missionary work in Tanzania on the one hand and in Lapland on the other hand.

The wider Church and individual parishes must consider and adapt, when possible, the implicit evangelization contained in the religious culture and customs of those evangelized, tapping into the traditions and history of different ethnic and social groups. Something similar applies to the use of technological means of communication — smart phones, the Internet, tablets, and so on. They change the way we learn, as we move away from a book culture that once dominated educational methods of teaching. They also require that we adapt and use their positive aspects to evangelize. This is well stated in the *National Directory for Catechesis*. It says, "The revolution in information technology provides the Church with unprecedented new ways to proclaim the Gospel in the United States" (p. 25).

The shift occurring in today's technological and media revolution influences the way we learn, think, and act. Everything seems instantaneous, whether it is a parent needing to talk to a child on a cell phone four or five times each day or two teenagers needing to text their friends multiple times each hour.

The digital revolution affects the way the brain filters thoughts. If people are used to instant results, how do they respond to the slow pace of some Church music and liturgy? Saying this doesn't imply that Catholics need to change their liturgy to accommodate modern times, but it points to a fundamental challenge that we must consider, if we hope to effectively evangelize our culture. Why? Because evangelization happens not only in words but also in the style of our lives, and in the space where we communicate. In considering this challenge, we must remember that we celebrate the liturgy to worship and praise God, which is at odds with the culture's need to be entertained.

3. What Is the New Evangelization?

Changing situations worldwide led Blessed John Paul II to call for a new evangelization and inspired Pope Benedict XVI to continue what he began, leading to the call for an international Synod of Bishops on the new evangelization in 2012.

The initial impetus to focus on the new evangelization came in Pope Paul VI's *On Evangelization in the Modern World*, but the direct call for it came from Pope John Paul II in a homily he delivered to the Polish people at the Shrine of the Holy Cross in Mogila, Poland, in June 1979. There, he called for a new agenda for the Church's evangelizing and missionary responsibilities.

In this address, John Paul II said that the time for a new evangelization had arrived. Four years after he gave this address in Poland, he again called for a new evangelization when speaking to the Latin American bishops. On this occasion, he emphasized that Latin America did not have to be re-evangelized. Rather, he called for a new evangelization that was "new in ardor, methods, and expression" (opening address of CELAM, March 9, 1983). These words sum up the main dynamic of the new evangelization. John Paul II continued to speak about it on many occasions (cf. Father James A. Wehner, S.T.D., *The Evangelization Equation*, 2011, Emmaus Road Publishing).

The New Evangelization

Blessed John Paul II used the terminology of the new evangelization to challenge the Church to reawaken her efforts to increase missionary and evangelical activity. In light of this, Pope Benedict XVI called the XIII Synod of Bishops, dedicated to the "New Evangelization for the Transmission of the Christian Faith." A preparatory document, a *Lineamenta*, sent out to prepare for this assembly reiterated John Paul II's challenge to awaken a new ardor, methods, and expression in evangelizing the changing world. It said:

> Consequently, the new evangelization is not a matter of redoing something which has been inadequately done or has not achieved its purpose, as if the new activity were an implicit judgment on the failure of the first evangelization. Nor is the new evangelization taking up the first evangelization again, or simply repeating the past. Instead, it is the courage to forge new paths in responding to the changing circumstances and conditions facing the Church in her call to proclaim and live the Gospel today. (Ch. 1, n. 5)

Quoting John Paul's encyclical *On the Permanent Validity of the Church's Missionary Mandate* (RM), this preparatory document (Ch. 1, n. 5) said:

> "Today all Christians, the particular Churches and the universal Church, are called to have the same courage that inspired the missionaries of the past, and the same readiness to listen to the voice of the Spirit." (Cf. RM, December 7, 1990, 30 AAS 83 [1991] 276)

Then, the preparatory document (Ch. 1, n. 5, emphasis in original) says that John Paul II later clarified his notion of the new evangelization, when he commented,

> "The Church today ought to take *a giant step forward* in her evangelization effort, and enter into *a new stage of history* in her missionary dynamism. In a world where the lessening of distance

makes the world increasingly smaller, the Church community ought to strengthen the bonds among its members, exchange vital energies and means, and commit itself as a group to a unique and common mission of proclaiming and living the Gospel." (John Paul II, *On the Vocation and the Mission of the Lay Faithful in the Church and in the World* [CL], December 30, 1988, 35: AAS 81 [1989] 458)

The new evangelization is not the same as a re-evangelization. In his address to CELAM, quoted above, when calling for a new evangelization, Blessed John Paul II said that it does not demand a re-evangelizing. It requires a new evangelization — new in its ardor, methods, and expression.

The preparatory document says, "Consequently, the new evangelization is not a matter of redoing something which has been inadequately done or has not achieved its purpose. . . . Instead, it is the courage to forge new paths in responding to the changing circumstances and conditions facing the Church in her call to proclaim and live the Gospel today" (Ch. 1, n. 5).

In lands that were formerly evangelized, the new evangelization focuses on beginning with the many rich values left in place as a consequence of the original sharing of God's Word. It aims at complementing them, while at the same time correcting their shortcomings.

The difference between these two expressions can be clarified by concrete illustrations. When an adult is evangelized prior to Baptism or a child is baptized, the baptismal seal marks the person as a child of God, raised to a supernatural life. This first evangelization and baptism begins the lifelong process of conversion, and the person continues to be evangelized throughout life. Hence, once baptized, a man or woman *is not re-evangelized*. Rather, one's faith can be renewed or deepened through what John Paul II calls *the new evangelization*. Today, what is needed is not a re-evangelization, as if the first evangelization received prior to Baptism did not take. What is needed is a new evangelization.

The new evangelization is deeply spiritual, and it concerns itself with developing a new ardor, enthusiasm, dynamism, and zeal in spreading the message of Jesus. It focuses on finding new methods to communicate Jesus' words in our highly secular and relativistic world, which rapidly moves toward universal globalization. It acknowledges new environments and new circumstances in which to evangelize. Jesus calls Christians to bring his Word into this changing world and to transform it from within through his teaching.

To consider the new evangelization in our country, the United States Bishops' Committee on Evangelization and Catechesis issued a document in 2012 entitled *Disciples Called to Witness: The New Evangelization*. It focuses on the New Evangelization in the current cultural context. It looks at its historical context and stresses the importance of witness and key outreach components. It says,

> The New Evangelization is a call to each person to deepen his or her own faith, have confidence in the Gospel, and possess a willingness to share the Gospel. It is a personal encounter with the person of Jesus, which brings peace and joy. The New Evangelization provides the lens through which people experience the Church and world around them. . . . Evangelization is the essence of the Church's identity. (Part I)

This document underlines the vital role that the sacraments, especially the Eucharist and Reconciliation, play in the evangelization process.

The "Mustard Seed" of the New Evangelization

Joseph Cardinal Ratzinger, in an address to catechists and religion teachers (December 12, 2000), speaks of progressive worldwide attempts to dechristianize society. He reiterates that the erosion of fundamental human values follow from taking Christ out of culture. In this context, he speaks of a new evangelization. In so doing, he alludes to the temptation to impatience, saying that our modern world wants instant results, which cannot be expected when sharing the Word of God. The message of Christ takes time to filter into one's soul, under the movement of the Holy Spirit.

The future pope goes on to say that we easily forget that conversion happens in God's time, not our own. Nonetheless, we must plant the seed. He uses the image of the mustard seed of the Gospels (Mark 4:30-32), where Jesus describes its slow growth to maturity. He applies this image of the growth of the mustard seed to the slow growth of the early Church, motivated by the seeds of martyrdom, and points out that gradually the Gospel spread throughout the world.

Cardinal Ratzinger then relates this slow but steady growth of a seed to the new evangelization, for conversion, like the kingdom of God, is a gradual process. According to him, the new evangelization is highly spiritual and will not succeed by new and dynamic methods alone.

The most basic evangelical method involves prayer, where the wider Church, parish, and individual evangelists put the results in God's hands, offering their personal efforts according to the designs and intent of the risen Lord. This requires patience and sacrifice.

The New Evangelization: An Integrated Perspective

The Father sent Jesus to proclaim a kingdom of forgiveness, peace, and justice. After his resurrection and ascension, Jesus sent the Holy Spirit to guide his Church in the way of salvation, the ultimate goal of all evangelizing activities. We evangelize, not only to praise and honor God, but to lead all people to the salvation won by Jesus through his death on the cross.

Consequently, to achieve the purpose for which it was initiated by the Father himself, evangelization must be pastorally and theologically integrated. This means that it must have a *Christological* focus, centering on the risen Christ. He accomplished our redemption and sent the Holy Spirit. Communion with Jesus is an important goal of the new evangelization. It must have a *pneumatic* perspective, recognizing the vital role that the Holy Spirit plays in all evangelizing activities. This is something that Catholics have not focused on sufficiently in catechesis. At the same time, evangelization must have an *ecclesiological* orientation, recognizing the fact that Catholic evangelization comes through the ecclesial community, the Church, by the power of the Holy Spirit. In addition, the new evangelization can never be a "me and Jesus thing." It also means that the new evangelization must be *Trinitarian* and *biblically* based, with the Church as the final judge of how the Word of God and the Church's living Tradition are the ultimate fonts of God's revelation. Finally, the Church keeps alive the *soteriological* goal of evangelization that is oriented toward our eternal goal, eternal happiness with God in heaven.

If we neglect any of these elements, the new evangelization is incomplete. Together, they form a unified whole, where the kingdom of God is partially realized here and fully realized in heaven.

The New Evangelization: Two Audiences

Blessed John Paul II and Pope Benedict XVI had two particular audiences in mind when they spoke of the new evangelization.

The *first audience* includes the mission to regions or countries that once had the Gospel preached to them and formerly practiced the Catholic faith but no longer practice it to any extent. We find instances of this in certain areas of South America and Europe, among others.

The new evangelization is a new proclamation of the Word of God to such places and countries where the Gospel was once celebrated and preached and needs reinvigoration and a new proclamation.

The *second audience* relates more to individuals than to groups, countries, or lands. It includes those who have been instructed in the Gospel and were Catholic for a time but now left the Church or no longer practice the faith. These include fallen-away Catholic parishioners and those beyond the parish. Parish members must be concerned also with alienated Catholics and those who no longer practice the faith for whatever reason.

The new evangelization is the new Catholic agenda because of the challenges presented to the Church today. Evangelization underlies all ministries and energizes the Christian life. We cannot be disciples without evangelizing. Convinced of Jesus' mission and ministry, we accept the new evangelization as our calling and open our hearts to the working of the Holy Spirit, as he invites us to follow Christ's missionary calling.

Confronted with worldly challenges, we strive to share Jesus' Good News in a meaningful and balanced way. The Great Commandment to love God and our neighbor is at the heart of our parish mission. All personal and parish renewal begins here.

4. Why the New Evangelization? Pastoral Reflections and Action Steps

To appreciate the new evangelization, it helps to reflect on it. The following points and action steps can be considered individually or with family members, school groups, or at parish meetings.

Pastoral Reflections

a. If someone asked you to describe how evangelization happens in your parish, what would you say?

b. What is the new evangelization? Why does the Church need a "new" evangelization? How is the new evangelization different from a re-evangelization?

c. Why do you think evangelization must be holistic, involving all parish ministries?

d. How does a greater appreciation of the new evangelization in a parish help parishioners better recognize their role as Christian evangelizers in the world, neighborhood, and marketplace?

Action Steps

a. Pastoral leaders need to develop a comprehensive plan to educate parishioners about the new evangelization.

b. Consider developing a short course of six one-hour sessions on the "why and what" of the new evangelization. Or use a video-based program on evangelization, such as "Sharing Christ," available at www.ChristLife.org.

c. Create a way for the parish to read and discuss Pope Paul VI's *On Evangelization in the Modern World*. For example, serialize the document in the parish bulletin and ask families and ministries to discuss each segment. Hold a parish-wide opening session to orient people to the process and a closing session where people can share what they learned.

d. Create a "New Evangelization" page on the parish website. Urge parishioners to frequent the site. Post links to all of the Vatican and USCCB documents. The page should include short instructions on evangelization, personal testimonies, the schedule of parish evangelistic activities, and so on.

Chapter Two

The Parish, the Kingdom, and the New Evangelization

Parishes evangelize because they are Christian communities, and Jesus commanded his followers to act in his name. To better appreciate the call of a parish, we consider Jesus' call to the kingdom of God and discipleship. To do this, we divide this chapter into six sections. The first considers the biblical basis for evangelization and the kingdom, while the second looks at Jesus and the kingdom. Section three reflects on the parish, the Church, and the kingdom of God, and section four examines healing, reconciliation, and the parish. Section five looks at discipleship and the kingdom, and the sixth section offers pastoral reflections and action steps.

We begin with the story of Millie.

Word came to a downtown parish that Millie, a bag lady, died and requested Catholic burial. Shortly before the funeral liturgy began, the priest heard noise in the church. Looking out from the sacristy, he saw beggars, alcoholics, bag ladies, and other street people assembling for the service.

The church was nearly filled. Unable to explain what was happening, after the Gospel, the priest discarded his prepared homily, walked among the congregation, and said, "Welcome! Why are all of you here? Who was this woman?"

A beggar responded, "Millie was the kindest person I knew. I loved her. She was good to me." An alcoholic continued, "That's right; she taught me about Jesus and gave me her coat when I was cold." The bag ladies nodded in approval. They all loved Millie, the "Saint of the Streets." That's why they came.

Street people knew Millie, even if parish ministers did not. Sharing her possessions with the poor spoke to them of God.

1. Biblical Basis for Evangelization and Kingdom

Millie's story reminds us of the episode in the Nazareth synagogue when Jesus said, "He has sent me to bring the good news to the poor, to proclaim liberty to captives and to the blind new sight, to set the downtrodden free, to proclaim the Lord's year of favour" (Luke 4:18; JB). Jesus' words are the heart of the kingdom, the goal of evangelization. What, then, is the kingdom of God that Jesus proclaimed?

The biblical terms for kingdom are *malkuth* in Hebrew and *basileia* in Greek. Sometimes they are translated into English as "reign" or "rule." But these words fail to capture the full impact of the biblical use.

The Hebrew and Greek words imply the power symbolized by a strong ruler or king. Such power included the submission of a servant to a master. Jesus turned this meaning on its head by using it in a radical way. He applied a paradoxical twist to its meaning for the follower of Christ: Power means service. He said, "You call me Master and Lord, and rightly; so I am. If I, then, the Lord and Master, have washed your feet, you should wash each other's feet" (John 13:13-14; JB).

Kingdom does not imply "king" in the sense that it gives precedence to a male figure. When using "kingdom," we accept, as Jesus did, the total equality of man and woman, young and old, servant and master.

As St. Paul says in Galatians,

> You are, all of you, [children] of God through faith in Christ Jesus. All baptised in Christ, you have all clothed yourselves in Christ, and there are no more distinctions between Jew and Greek, slave and free, male and female, but all of you are one in Christ Jesus. (Galatians 3:26-28; JB)

God's kingdom can be described as *God's healing presence.* The Hebrew and Christian Scriptures indicate how God's presence frees people from brokenness and sin and moves them toward health and wholeness. The goal of God's kingdom is to give life and freedom, not to hold people in death and bondage.

2. Jesus and the Kingdom

The parish evangelizes as the first Christians did by proclaiming the kingdom of God. There is nothing new about this. *What is new is the parish's need to find new ways and a new spirit in its evangelizing efforts.* Evangelization, from Jesus' time until today, is an essential aspect of being a Christian. His words to the apostles and disciples before he ascended into heaven are meant also for us. He said, "Go therefore, and make disciples of all the nations" (Matthew 28:19; JB).

Parishes evangelize because they continue Jesus' mission and ministry, one reflected in the first words written in any Gospel. Mark says, "The beginning of the Good News about Jesus Christ, the Son of God . . ." (Mark 1:1; JB). These words parallel the words of Genesis, "In the beginning when God created the heavens and the earth . . ." (1:1; NRSV). Genesis describes the birth of creation, whereas Mark describes the new birth of humankind into a redeemed People of God brought about through Jesus' dying and rising to atone for the sin of Adam.

Parish members evangelize because they have been born into this new life through Baptism. Through it, we become members of Christ's body, disciples of the risen Lord, and advocates for the kingdom of God, God's gift to us.

The kingdom of God is the key to the understanding of Jesus' mission and the parish's call to be disciples of his kingdom. This is the reason why we evangelize (*General Directory for Catechesis*, n. 34). A personal experience helps us better appreciate the kingdom.

Ben spent much of his time ministering to poor people. He resided in a two-room apartment in the inner city, surviving without salary or benefits. He had an old truck and a tremendous faith in God.

He called me two weeks before Christmas, saying that the poor in Appalachia were in particularly difficult conditions this year because the government had cut back certain assistance programs. He asked me to get him food, clothes, and blankets to fill his truck so that he could help them this Christmas. I obtained the items he requested.

Several days after Christmas, we planned to go out for lunch. I met him at his apartment. His austere surroundings struck me. With his simple mountain furniture, it was almost as if a cabin had been moved to the city. While looking around, my eyes settled on several black-and-white photographs hanging on the wall. The center one showed three poorly dressed women, several children, some chickens, and a dog standing in the dirt before a large, rusted tin shed. The shed was about 30 feet long, 15 feet deep, and 8 feet high. It protruded from a mountain, which formed the back wall.

"Who are those women, and where is that shed?" I asked. Ben replied, "That's where we celebrated Christmas this year. Inside the shed, I gave out the supplies you obtained for me. The old woman in the middle lived in a cave until three years ago. The other women and children were abandoned. They got together and started living in the shed, which the coal companies once used for storage."

Ben continued, "I want you to hear something." He picked up an old tape recorder and located the place he wanted on the tape. "This," he said, "is from our Christmas celebration in the tin shed." I listened. The guitarist was a bit flat and the singers off key, but from that tape came joy, peace, and love like I have never experienced on any professionally produced tape. Then it struck me: "That's the way Jesus was born!"

Jesus came among the poor in an out-of-the-way place. His first visitors were shepherds, who often had reputations as thieves. Some stole food and other necessities to support themselves and their families. Together, like the poor of the gospels, the Appalachian poor celebrated God's love and renewed their hope by living again the story of Jesus' birth.

Then something else hit me. For the first time I realized that the infancy narratives in Matthew and Luke describing Jesus' birth and early life were meant to introduce a key theme at the heart of the Gospels — the kingdom of God. These stories are introductions to Jesus' kingdom message. They tell us how Jesus was rejected, cast out, and broken, not only in his last days but also from the beginning of his life.

The story of Ben invites us to see that Jesus accepted an impoverished state to show us the depth of God's love. Because Jesus, the Son of God, accepted human brokenness that the New Testament describes, we can be confident that God is present in the hurting, broken conditions of every one of us. The Christian God is a God who loves everyone, but is present especially when we are hurting and broken, helping us become whole and holy.

Today, as in Jesus' time, many hurting parishioners struggle to survive. Whatever the brokenness, their stories of pain and grief invite parish ministers to reflect God's love of every person.

The parish community is the bearer of Jesus' Good News. In so doing, it embodies the relationship between evangelization and the kingdom, reflected in Pope Paul VI's words: "There is no true evangelization if the name, the teaching, the life, the promises, the kingdom and the mystery of Jesus of Nazareth, the Son of God, are not proclaimed" (*On Evangelization in the Modern World*, n. 22).

To better appreciate the meaning of "kingdom," Scripture reminds us that:

- God sent Jesus.
- He knew poverty.
- His mission was to proclaim the kingdom of God.
- He did this through his ministry — namely, his life, words, and deeds.
- The kingdom is directed toward the poor, whether they are experiencing economic, physical, psychological, or spiritual poverty.
- The kingdom is present when healing, reconciliation, and forgiveness occur.

Jesus taught us that poverty is an evil to be overcome, not a condition to be maintained. He proclaimed Good News to the poor, salvation to sinners, and hope to those without hope. Therefore, while God is a friend of the poor, this same God calls every parish to help root out the causes of poverty. Jesus gives testimony to God's plan in becoming one like us in everything, except sin.

Poverty, Healing, and Reconciliation

In becoming one like us, Jesus was born in poverty and experienced forms of economic, physical, psychological, and spiritual poverty. In his adult years as a wandering preacher, he was not bound to material possessions, saying of himself, "the Son of Man has nowhere to lay his head" (Matthew 8:20; JB).

Jesus also accepted physical poverty, which implies bodily suffering. The stories of his birth hint at the pain Jesus experienced in the difficult situation of his birth. Jesus' agony and crucifixion are supreme symbols of his willingness to embrace physical poverty.

Jesus' psychological poverty must have been intense. Throughout his life, people misunderstood him. They threw him out of the Temple, opposed his teaching, harassed his disciples, and accused him of blasphemy. Judas betrayed him and Peter denied him. Jesus agonized in the Garden and died on the cross. Psychological or emotional poverty permeated his life.

Jesus was not exempt from spiritual poverty. Sin brings about spiritual poverty, for it sets us at variance with our true purpose. Jesus was without sin but suffered the effects of original sin and the personal sins of humans. He accepted the condition of human loneliness and alienation to save the world.

Consciousness of his mission gave meaning to Jesus' life. But when near death, even Jesus questioned the meaning of what was happening to him, when he cried out, "My God, my God, why have you deserted me?" (Mark 15:34; JB).

His rejection and isolation lead to questions like the one he uttered to his Father. But when despair tempted him, he turned to God, saying, "Father, into your hands I commit my spirit" (Luke 23:46; JB). Christian faith tells us we must do the same. How can pastoral leaders help those suffering from spiritual poverty see this connection?

The Gospels indicate clearly that Jesus assumed the human condition. God's presence, reflected in Jesus' teaching on the kingdom, was central to his life and ministry. He became poor to vanquish poverty. His example affords hope for anyone immersed in poverty, for Jesus teaches that poverty is never the end. He died for our sins and teaches us that we must forgive one another.

3. The Parish, the Church, and the Kingdom of God

Jesus' mission and ministry continue in the Church, his mystical body. This realization dawned on the disciples at Pentecost as the Holy Spirit illuminated them, helping them see the Christian community as responsible to proclaim the kingdom under the guidance of the Spirit.

The parish does this through its corporate and individual ministry of teaching, good example, worship, prayer, and social concern.

Thus, the Church helps bring God's kingdom to completion. As Blessed John Paul II says in *On the Permanent Validity of the Church's Missionary Mandate*, "Likewise, one may not separate the kingdom from the Church. It is true that the Church is not an end unto herself, since she is ordered toward the kingdom of God of which she is the seed, sign and instrument" (n. 18). Like the life of Jesus, the Church is directed toward the poor and broken, offering them healing, reconciliation, and forgiveness. The spirit of the kingdom of God, so powerfully preserved in the Beatitudes and the Sermon on the Mount, continues to inspire us to follow Jesus as disciples (Matthew 5:3-12; CCC 1716).

Poverty Today

Today's people suffer forms of poverty that Jesus experienced. The Catholic parish must bring help and solace to such people who struggle to find meaning in devastating situations. This means that pastoral ministers must bring spiritual meaning, and human support, to the economically, physically, psychologically, or spiritually poor. These conditions take distinct forms today.

Much of the world is *economically impoverished* as millions of people, lacking adequate food, clothing and shelter, are left to a cruel fate. Christians can help by giving them money and material goods or by volunteering their services. This kind of giving, good and necessary in itself, aids many people. But it can subtly camouflage real poverty issues, for charity will never alleviate poverty; only justice will.

More and more Christians are accepting the kingdom's call to work for justice and oppose the economic, social, and political systems that keep people impoverished. The presence of God calls Christian political leaders, business executives, workers, and family members to carry out their mission to help alleviate economic poverty. The United States bishops, in *Sharing Catholic Social Teaching: Challenges and Directions*, spoke of this obligation in these words: "We believe that every person is precious, that people are more important than things, and that the measure of every institution is whether it threatens or enhances the life and dignity of the human person" (p. 4). In this regard, Christians must be concerned for all poor people, including the illegal immigrants who enter our country.

Physical poverty refers to bodily impairments caused by such things as sickness, accidents, handicaps of birth, or the aging process. The Gospel recounts many stories of Jesus healing those who suffered from physical poverty. The kingdom proclaimed by his life and ministry promises God's presence through his Church to those suffering from physical poverty.

Marcia is a dormitory placement coordinator at a large university. Seven students came to her office the first day of the fall semester demanding to be moved from the dormitory to which they were assigned. "Why?" Marcia inquired. Bill — a strong, athletic man — spoke for the group: "The people there are different. Some don't speak right, others can't walk, still others are hunched over." Marcia realized immediately that the students had been assigned to the dormitory of people with handicapping conditions.

She told them that she would get their rooms changed, but that it would take about a month. Sue, one of the seven students, was adamant, saying, "We want out now!" Finally, the group reluctantly agreed to stay in this dorm until changes could be arranged. They were to check back later with Marcia.

About three weeks later, Marcia was eating dinner in a popular restaurant. She heard laughing and hilarity in an adjoining room. Looking through the door, she saw the seven students who had come to her office earlier. Sue was helping a handicapped girl cut her food. Another assisted a young man with his vegetables. After some time, Bill raised a glass and said, "Let's toast God for bringing us together." Then, turning to a severely handicapped student, he said, "Happy birthday, Ed!"

Marcia waited for the students to return to her office. One month passed, then a few more, and finally the year ended. They never returned to change their dormitory. These students learned from the Gospel message: "Happy are the poor in spirit" (Matthew 5:3; JB). The physically handicapped students taught the other seven about life.

Catholic parishes and individual evangelizers can learn valuable lessons from this story. When Christians reach out to help the needy, more than the handicapped are blessed.

Psychological poverty is also widespread in modern society. Life's fast pace, the pressures to balance work and family life, the widespread use of drugs, and other social ills drive people to emotional upheaval and illness. Too often life becomes a series of chores to be done rather than an exciting mystery to be celebrated. With this in mind, how can pastoral ministers help a teenager or parent, ravaged by drugs, find meaning in life, when so much around them is falling apart? Doing this is an aspect of the new evangelization.

Some years ago, Bill, a college student, responded negatively to my efforts to help him in class. During the first four weeks, he missed most of his classes and most assignments. When I asked why, he said, "I'm not interested in this class. I took it because I have to. After school, I work to pay for my education. This takes much of my time."

Halfway through the term, I talked to him again. By this time, he was doing even less work and rarely came to class. I told him I couldn't pass him unless he improved. He became adamant and said he didn't care. Finally, I tossed my grade book on the desk and said, "Bill, I don't care about your grades, but I do care about you. Won't you please let me be your friend?"

Hearing this, this large young man fell on me and sobbed like a baby. Finally he looked up and said, "Father, you are the first person in my life that ever asked me to be his friend." He never missed another class, made up his work, and got a "B."

Bill suffered from a gnawing loneliness that paralyzed him in an almost meaningless life. He needed encouragement and a friend. Many people, like Bill, exist. They cry out for someone to reach out to them. Evangelization gives this kind of witness to help further God's kingdom.

People who suffer mental breakdowns or are mentally handicapped also experience psychological poverty. They need understanding but also invite us to gain a deeper understanding of the Gospel message.

Spiritual poverty is rampant, as people search desperately for meaning. The deepest spiritual poverty is sin, which interferes with the God-human relationship. By freely turning away from God through mortal sin, people cut themselves off from the deepest wellsprings of grace and meaning.

Sins committed years ago often continue to gnaw at people. Some believe their sins are unforgivable. Failing to appreciate Jesus' Good News of forgiveness, they live in quiet desperation.

A pastoral minister sat daily with a man belonging to no church. Near death, he lingered on. One afternoon, he shared with her something he did years ago. He cried. The pastoral minister said that she believed God forgave him. He answered, "Do you really believe God forgave me?"

"Yes," the woman replied. Great peace came over him, as they prayed for God's forgiveness. He died a few hours after she left.

Because of the world's sinful condition and life's imperfections, we experience other kinds of spiritual poverty as well. One is spiritual meaninglessness, indicated by hollowness in our lives. In a world where money, power, and sex take precedence over justice, peace, and love, our deepest needs for affection, security, happiness, and meaning often go unattended.

Life's Priorities

The spiritual yearning for love, understanding, relaxation, and play will not go away. Life is out of hand when play or visiting a friend becomes a chore in an appointment book, carried out on a schedule. The ultimate cannot be programmed. No wonder the Hebrew Scriptures say, "Remember the Sabbath day and keep it holy" (Exodus 20:8; JB). The first creation account tells us, "God blessed the seventh day and made it holy, because on that day he had rested after all his work of creating" (Genesis 2:3; JB). These passages remind us to take time for God, ourselves, and others. Genesis gives us a clue on how to put life in better balance. Keep Sunday holy, praise God, pray, enjoy family and friends, relax, and have fun.

I learned about life's priorities from Sam, a student in a college course. After the first day of class, Sam, a handsome, strong-looking student, approached me. "Father, I'll have to miss one class every other week. Is that okay?" I replied, "Not really, unless you have a good reason." Sam explained that he had a rare blood disease and came close to death two years before.

"Every other week they bring me to the hospital and replace my blood, so I can live for two more weeks." I was stunned as I looked at this man with the physique of a football player. I said, "Sam, you'd better miss class every other week."

As the class progressed, Sam's maturity impressed the students. He never mentioned his ailment. A month before the end of the semester, he wrote a reflection paper. After reading it, I asked him to share it with the class. The day he did, Sam began by rolling up his long-sleeved shirt that always covered his arms. Then he bent his arms and said, "Look at my arms! They are like leather."

As he pounded them, they resembled the sleeves of a leather jacket. "They are like this," he continued, "because hospital personnel have stuck hundreds of needles into them to give me blood. Now my arms will take no more needles, and they must find other places in my body to put the needles." Shocked by the appearance of Sam's arms and by his initial comments, the students listened in rapt attention to his story. At one point, he picked up the reflection paper he wrote for me and read:

What does life mean to you? Is life something you put on every morning like your clothes and walk out the door not giving it another thought? Or is life something you put on like your clothes and walk out the door making the most of every second, of every hour, of every day?

The date is September 12, 19--. The location is a hospital in St. Louis, Missouri.

As I walk down the hospital corridor, I see a young girl smile at me. We start talking, and I tell her about my illness and she says she has a tumor at the edge of her brain. Tomorrow she will have surgery. Sally is only 12 and knows she will either be okay or have a malignancy or come out of surgery paralyzed. It seems so unreal, for she is so young. I almost wish Jesus was there and I could beat on his chest and ask, "Why?"

Sally didn't expect to see me the next morning. They wheel her around the corner where I stand and stop the cart. Sally puts out her arms, we hug, and she looks at me as if to say, "I'm ready." Then they wheel her into the elevator.

When I turn from the elevator, I see the radiator. I kick it so hard that if it wasn't attached to the wall, I would have kicked it right out the window. When I kick the radiator, I look up at the ceiling and shout, "Why? She's only twelve! And why did I nearly die several years ago? One day I played in an all-star football game; two days later I woke up sick, and ten days later I discovered I had a rare blood ailment."

Sally is fine today, and I continue to amaze the doctors. Through my experiences I learned something about the "why" of suffering. Even more, I learned to appreciate life. My message is simple: "Make the most of life! Live it to the fullest." For there are people of all ages who would give anything just to walk up the street, just to live a near-normal life.

I know the meaning of suffering, for I have almost died four times. Through suffering I yearn for life. Nothing means more to me than to wake up to see the light and the smog, for I have learned to appreciate just being alive.

Sam had a tremendous influence on the students. He lived a hopeful message. I never saw him after the semester ended, but his words remain with me, especially his final remarks on that class day: "Miracles do happen! They aren't caused by you or me, but by God. So trust God, no matter what might happen." Faith, like Sam's, roots spiritual meaning, which is the foundation of Catholic evangelization and human activities.

The message of Sam's story is that no effective evangelization happens unless it is rooted in the spiritual. If dioceses, parishes, and individuals live the spiritual message of the Gospels, Christians will be inspired to counter today's secular message with a God-centered message that offers ultimate meaning in a functional world. The kingdom of God happens when people turn away from the alienation caused by functional gods to discover healing, health, and wholeness in God's love and human compassion.

4. Healing, Reconciliation, and the Parish

Evangelization demands a reconciling community. We hear of our responsibility to forgive, over and over again, as we assemble for the Sunday liturgy and pray the most powerful Christian prayer, the Our Father (Matthew 6:9-13; CCC 2776).

Healing, reconciliation, and forgiveness result from the presence of God's kingdom. When these happen, God is there. To learn to what degree a parish, school, family, or individual lives the kingdom message, one might observe their willingness to reconcile or forgive.

Since the kingdom of God is gauged by forgiveness, God invites us to re-create society. For Christians, this means the constant need to be reconciled. At times, people find it difficult to recognize Jesus' example of forgiveness in our parishes. Some parishioners are disillusioned at the lack of charity in Church leaders who are supposed to symbolize Jesus' message.

Frequently, people working in a parish are turned off by politics, infighting, and turf building. While they operate under the banner of Christ, the results of God's healing and forgiveness may not be evident.

Once I moderated a pastoral council meeting in a large parish that was split into two rival factions. We met on Sunday afternoon at a retreat setting. After fifteen minutes of haggling, group hostility made it impossible to discuss significant issues. Eventually, I interrupted the meeting and said, "Stop! Look at what's happening. Since I am coordinating this meeting, I recommend that you choose one of two options. First, go home and enjoy the beautiful afternoon. There is no need to continue this way. Second, go aside by yourselves for several hours, ask

God to enlighten you, pray for forgiveness, and then reassemble. Then we'll see how you feel. We won't celebrate the Eucharist together this afternoon, if we refuse to forgive one another and be civil. If we do, what meaning will the Mass have for us?"

I asked which option they preferred. They refused to admit defeat and did not want to go home. So they went off for several hours. At 5:00 p.m., the group gathered in the chapel and discussed their attitudes and actions. They wanted to celebrate Mass, eat dinner together, and try to have a Christian meeting that evening. I felt God's presence within the group moving them to reconciliation, so I agreed and celebrated Mass. After dinner, we met from 7:30 to 9:00 p.m. Their outlook had changed. I attribute it to the power of the reconciling Christ in their midst.

The new evangelization focuses on the kingdom, which goes beyond Church membership. Parishes need to strive to become reconciling communities and invite the members to evangelize others as reconcilers. An evangelist is a reconciling person, reaching out to the poor, whatever their religion, nationality, or economic condition, and inviting them to experience God's love. Catholic evangelization helps people be reconciled with themselves, others, and God.

If evangelization becomes too ecclesial or Church-centered, it misses Jesus' focus on the kingdom and his desire to reconcile all creation to God and runs the risk of developing into narrow, one-sided proselytization. Catholic evangelists invite others to become Church members, not to swell parish ranks, but because they believe that the Catholic Church is the best way for them to become Christlike and thus more fully human.

5. Discipleship and the Kingdom

In the Gospel of *Mark* we read:

> In those days Jesus came from Nazareth of Galilee and was baptized by John in the Jordan. And just as he was coming up out of the water, he saw the heavens torn apart and the Spirit descending like a dove on him. And a voice came from heaven, "You are my Son, the Beloved; with you I am well pleased." (Mark 1: 9-11; NRSV)

A close relationship exists between this passage, the Pentecost experience — when the Spirit descended upon Jesus' disciples (Acts 2:1-4) —

Christian Baptism, and the call to discipleship. The message contained here is at the heart of evangelization and of being a disciple.

Mark proclaimed Jesus as God's Son (Mark 1:11). This initiated the hearers into Jesus' evangelizing activity — namely, his proclamation of God's Good News of salvation. The passage in Acts, quoted above, is closely related to the one in Mark. On Pentecost, the Spirit descended upon the disciples, thus beginning the Church's mission to evangelize, to proclaim the saving reality of Jesus' dying and rising for the sins of the world. It, too, initiated the disciples' public ministry.

In Christian Baptism, the Spirit descended upon the baptized, thus initiating them into the Paschal Mystery. This action set the foundation for our response as Christian disciples. Throughout our lives, we grow into the meaning of our baptism. The latter begins a lifelong process. Baptism is not a once-for-all event. At whatever age it is received, it sets the stage for our public profession of Jesus as Lord. It symbolizes our call to serve as Christian disciples, who proclaim the Good News, as did Jesus' followers after Pentecost. The same Holy Spirit that descended upon Jesus and the disciples descends upon us at Baptism, setting the foundation for our response as disciples who evangelize others into God's love.

The *General Directory for Catechesis* (n. 15) says:

> Two thousand years ago [Jesus] proclaimed the Gospel in Palestine and sent the disciples to sow the Gospel in the world. Today, Jesus Christ, present in the Church through his Spirit, continues to scatter the word of the Father ever more widely in the field of the world.

Today's disciple scatters God's word to the ends of the earth. This can happen through a mother's love, a father's sacrifice, a friend's compassion, or a minister's dedicated service. It happens, also, through a computer specialist's dedicated efforts to bring modern techniques to Third World countries, a business person's just dealings with employees, a corporate executive's work to provide food for people in starving countries, a volunteer missionary's ministry in a devastated area, and the multiple efforts of people to reach out to the needy. In so doing, the modern disciple continues to share Jesus' Good News in the midst of sadness, fear, and anxiety. The person fulfills the Lord's calling by sharing hope, freedom, and healing with those he or she meets.

The disciple of any age continues Jesus' mission of proclaiming the kingdom of God, a kingdom that promises peace, salvation, and eternal life. Unlike earthly promises, the disciple shares God's word, knowing that the Lord of heaven and earth is always faithful. The Christian God is a God that cannot go back on the word of life, promised by Jesus, and sealed by his death and resurrection.

The Good News that evangelization proclaims believes firmly that every Christian is called to discipleship. This invitation, rooted in Baptism, is clarified through a lifelong conversion process. In accepting this call to discipleship, the follower of Christ knows that he or she will be guided by the Holy Spirit. As the *Catechism of the Catholic Church* (CCC) says, "the Spirit will now be with and in the disciples, to teach them and guide them 'into all the truth' (cf. Gen 1:2; Nicene Creed [DS 150]; Jn 14:17, 26; 16:13)" (n. 243). For this to happen, the disciples follow the master by taking up their cross and following him (Matthew 16:24).

The call to discipleship presents great challenges for parish ministers, for this calling is lived out in a society whose values often oppose those of Jesus. This contrast in values provides a fruitful way for a parish to exercise a prophetic function and to highlight the remarkable depth of Jesus' message.

While relativism, individualism, and secularism leave many feeling shallow, lonely, and lost, Jesus' message promises fulfillment and peace. The way of Christ is a fresh alternative to the tired, worn-out promises of a society that lives as if only today's pleasures count. The way of the Lord, proclaimed two thousand years ago, is the ever fresh, new way that the Christian disciple announces to the world.

To exercise the call to discipleship, pastoral ministers must take up their cross in the many challenges of society, family, and parish responsibilities. This means having a constant desire to grow in faith, hope, and charity. It requires an ongoing effort at conversion to a lifestyle that is generous, patient, and kind. It means the willingness to sacrifice for the truth, speak out against injustice, and use the gifts God has bestowed on us to build God's kingdom on earth.

Pastoral ministers as disciples and evangelists are persons of prayer and loyal to the teachings of Christ and the Church. They know who they are as Christians and are eager to share Jesus' message with others. Disciples also work with other Christian denominations and religious traditions to spread a message of truth and compassion.

Discipleship usually begins with good example shown in our family, God's crucible fostering faithful discipleship. The witness of Christians in the world reinforces these humble beginnings. In varied ways, Christian discipleship, rooted in evangelization and the kingdom of God, continues the salvific work of Jesus.

6. The Parish, the Kingdom, and the New Evangelization: Pastoral Reflections and Action Steps

Parish leaders can intensify their appreciation of the rich scope of the kingdom of God. To further its understanding and to see its connection with the new evangelization, we look more deeply to better understand our role as disciples of Jesus Christ.

Pastoral Reflections

a. If you are asked to clarify the meaning of the kingdom of God, how would you answer? How would you describe the relationship among the kingdom of God, the Church, the parish, and the new evangelization?

b. What are some ways that a parish can bring the healing graces of the kingdom to those suffering from each of the different kinds of poverty (economic, physical, psychological, and spiritual)?

c. What actions do you think a parish must take to become a reconciling community?

d. What must a parish do to encourage and equip parishioners to embrace their call to discipleship?

Action Steps

a. Pastoral leaders can conduct an assessment of the degrees of poverty (economic, physical, psychological, and spiritual) in the parish and local area. They might form a team of parishioners to survey the situation.

b. Challenge the parish to develop a plan to develop and implement several important but easy to implement ways of relieving poverty in the parish and surrounding area. Possibilities may include bringing nonperishable food to Mass every weekend for supplying local food pantries; providing the services of a part-time parish nurse; arranging for parish volunteers at local outreaches to the homeless; having qualified retirees help others with financial planning, and so on.

c. The parish needs to educate members about the nature of the Kingdom, the Church's teaching on social justice, and the meaning of discipleship. Options include:

- Offer a parish mission on the subject of "The Kingdom, Social Justice, and the New Evangelization."
- Provide educational opportunities on the kingdom, social justice, and discipleship. For example, consider using programs like JustFaith (www.justfaith.org) and/or the Catherine of Siena Institute (www.siena.org) to form parishioners as disciples and give them a heart for the poor.
- Post on the parish website teachings and links to websites on social justice, discipleship, and evangelization.

d. Consider establishing regular Adoration of the Blessed Sacrament to pray for the coming of the kingdom in the parish. Have specific prayer intentions for people, programs, and events.

Chapter Three

The Parish in Contemporary Culture: The Challenge to the New Evangelization

To better appreciate our challenge to be people of hope as pastoral leaders, this chapter looks at the new evangelization and contemporary culture in five sections. Section one addresses the basic goodness of the world, while the second section points out the challenges it affords. Section three looks at the five sectors of the world affecting the new evangelization. Section four considers the way media and technology are changing the culture. The final section offers pastoral reflections and action steps.

The wisdom of Blessed John Paul II, calling for a new evangelization, was influenced by his intense awareness of changing world circumstances. Like no other pope before him, his extensive travels and his rubbing shoulders with communists, capitalists, atheists, and various other groups put him in a unique position to recognize the challenges that modern culture presents to the Church. He recognized the opportunities for the Church to help civilization discover new spiritual meaning in the midst of pain and sorrow. He recognized that a greater awareness of the courage of the early martyrs in the face of suffering and death helps us see that there is hope in traumatic circumstances. He called for a new evangelization to discover new ways to bring Christ's message of hope to a changing world.

We begin with the story of Sue, Sarah, and Kim.

I had hoped to relax during the flight from Philadelphia, in the left bulkhead seat next to the aisle. Shortly before takeoff, the attendant seated a four-year-old girl beside me. Soon afterward, the attendant placed an older woman across the aisle.

The last thing I needed was a child gabbing during the entire flight. Instinctively, I slouched down into my seat to avoid conversation. Almost immediately, the child poked my arm and said, "I'm Sue, who are you?" Somewhat startled, I answered, "I'm Bob."

"Glad to meet you, Bob," she said. Then, pointing to a rag doll, the child continued, "This is Kim." After greeting "Kim," as I was ordered to do by the child, I disappeared further into my seat.

Prior to takeoff, Sue's chattering with Kim caused me to notice that the child had not buckled her seat belt. I said, "You have to buckle your seat belt."

"I don't know how; please buckle it for me," Sue replied. I fastened it and then closed my eyes again.

A few moments later, Sue again poked me saying, "You did it wrong; you didn't buckle up Kim." I apologized, as I watched Sue put Kim under her seat belt.

Just before the plane left the ground, a voice across the aisle asked me, "Is your name Bob?" After I said yes, the woman continued, "I'm Sarah, and I'm really scared; this is the first time I've been on a plane. I'm old, handicapped, and can't read or write. Will you buckle me up too?" So I buckled her up.

After the plane was in the air, Sarah looked toward the window and asked, "Can I take off this belt and look out the window?" I told her to wait until the pilot turned off the light, which indicated it was safe to move around the plane. When this happened a short time later, I told Sarah she could go to the window.

Excitedly, Sarah looked outside and said, "Bob, hurry over here and see what I see." I did so, and immediately Sarah continued, "What's that . . . that . . . that . . . and that?" pointing to clouds, hills, rivers, trees, and grass. After I told her what they were, Sarah looked puzzled and replied in a childlike, humble way, "No, it's not any of those things."

"What, then, is it?" I asked. Sarah said simply, "It's God's beautiful garden." I gulped and returned to my seat.

Sue, Sarah, Kim, and I conversed and laughed the rest of the trip. When I left them, I was refreshed. The fatigue was gone. Upon leaving the plane, they waved good-bye. At that moment, I knew that a deep part of three very different people touched a common chord, which sprung from our human oneness.

The woman's and child's simplicity renewed a childlike part of me. Sue's relationship with Kim and Sarah's view of the universe as God's beautiful garden touched my soul. They opened up a dimension of reality that I had forgotten.

The experience reaffirmed for me the basic goodness of the world, a fundamental Catholic teaching from which we begin to consider today's cultural challenges and to offer perspectives on the new evangelization.

1. The Basic Goodness of the World

The Catholic Tradition holds that the world is good but wounded. The first incarnation of God happened in creation, which Genesis describes in the first creation account (Genesis 1:1-2:4). Here, the sacred author tells us that God created the world and its inhabitants as good. Early people saw God's creation in this way, but they saw something more. They recognized the presence of evil, brokenness, and failure and wondered, "Why?"

The second creation account (Genesis 2:5ff.), telling the story of Adam and Eve, addresses the issue of sin and evil. Here, the sacred author asks, "Why does evil exist in the world?" The story indicates that after Adam and Eve sinned, God did not abandon them, and hints at the redemption of the human race. Catholic theology teaches that after the Fall, the world was wounded but not corrupted. We find reflections of God's presence in creation, life, and people. Consequently, Catholic spirituality includes nature as an important manifestation of God's loving presence.

Our good, yet wounded world needed redemption, which happened through the life, death, and resurrection of Jesus. This second incarnation of God in Jesus affords us hope and promises us eventual salvation. The risen Lord continues to live in the world, in the baptized, and in the Church. This belief is reflected by the U.S. bishops in the words of the *General Directory for Catechesis*: "Jesus, in the parable of the sower, proclaims the Good News that the Kingdom of God is near, notwithstanding the problems in the soil, the tensions, conflicts and difficulties of the world" (n. 15).

Consequently, Christians must approach culture and the new evangelization in a positive way. They search for God in nature, human experience, and the Church. As the *General Directory for Catechesis* says, "The Christian knows that every human event — indeed all reality — is marked by the creative activity of God which communicates goodness to all beings . . ." (n. 16).

The Christian pastoral minister needs to bring a positive, hope-filled message to a world that often has no roadmap, except that which materialism, relativism, and secularism provide. Their worldly pull affords significant challenges for Christians. The world pulls us into it and draws us away from God at the same time. In so doing, it creates a vacuum in our hearts that moves us to search for God. As this happens, we know instinctively that all earthly values cannot be relative, that material possessions and wealth alone cannot bring happiness, and that the hectic pace of society cannot be the answer.

The answer for which moderns search cannot be found in an idealized past or an unrealized future. Often, we fail to truly live in the present but instead continue to drain ourselves through work, superficial activities, and frenzied schedules. The same technology, which ushered in the contemporary era and shapes our priorities and values, invites us to take another look.

2. Challenges of Contemporary Culture

"In the light of the Gospel, the Church must appropriate all the positive values of culture and of cultures (cf. EN 20; CT 53) and reject those elements which impede development of the true potential of persons and peoples" (*General Directory for Catechesis*, n. 21).

Technology is a great gift. Used properly, it builds the earth and brings peace, justice, and freedom. It offers untold possibilities for good, when we root our lives in ultimate values (love, justice, and truth) and see it as a means to an end, not as an end in itself. It affords wonderful opportunities to build a better world through science, medicine, business, communication, research, and travel.

But these benefits have a flip side. The media stresses superficiality, relativism, possessions, money, sex, and power. These underlying values canonize a quantified, functional worldview that knows no variations and leaves little room for ultimate values. In any pastoral situation, these negative values must be brought to the consciousness of parishioners, so as to help them address the challenges they face.

Cultural values, ritualized in the media, affect family life. Often, our busy life resembles a television set. We turn it on in the morning, go-go-

go all day, take an occasional time-out for a commercial, eat, shop, love on the run, and turn it off to sleep after the eleven o'clock news. The next day we start all over again. Where is the joy in this? Without joy, how can we find any lasting meaning?

Some Christians, who live like this, rarely have time or take the time to unwind, enjoy nature, experience intimacy, pray, or keep Sunday as the Lord's Day. For them, Sunday exists to catch up on the week's chores, because quantifiable, functional values, like making money, have priority. With little depth in their lives, just surviving in the everyday becomes the goal.

Today's families need support from the parish, as they struggle to live happy lives, often with little help from society or family traditions that once established a solid set of values. They tread uncharted paths, influenced by television, digital communications, movies, music, books, and advertising. Amidst many pressures, families do remarkably well in sharing ultimate values, like intimacy and love, but secular pressures are great. It is easy for them to fall into the trap of functionalism without realizing it.

A Catholic second-grade schoolteacher who taught for more than forty years said,

> I never taught children before who were so spiritually deprived. Many experience the worst kind of spiritual deprivation. Their parents seldom pray with them or speak about God. Except for school time, many are in day care from 6:30 a.m. to 6:30 p.m. After this, parents shuffle them to fast-food restaurants and through shopping centers well into the evening. They get so many things to appease them that Christmas and Easter gifts have little meaning.

Marital stress, especially divorce, often devastates children. One third-grade boy said, "My daddy's latest girlfriend likes our hamster more than me." A sixth-grade religion teacher said, "By sixth grade, many kids build a wall around themselves. They have to be cool. To show emotion means running the risk of getting hurt." The new evangelization challenges pastoral ministers to help such children recognize that there is more to life than what they presently experience and to grow in faith in such circumstances. This is not easy and often requires the collective wisdom of pastoral ministers, parents, and other significant adults.

Many people assimilate value systems where success and status are more important than integrity. Few such individuals are joyful. They may be wealthy in the world's eyes, but poor in meaning, knowing little more than how to make a buck or control people. When materialism predominates in a home, children pick up its subtle message, exemplified by a seventh-grade girl who, after hearing Jesus' story, replied, "Did you say that Jesus was a carpenter? How do you really expect me to follow him if he was only a carpenter?" This girl was at an age where she began to look for deeper meaning in her life. Observing her, it was obvious that she showed little joy and less deep meaning in the presence of her designer clothes. About the only thing she desired was new fancy clothes and a rich lifestyle.

Children need time with their parents, spent in relaxed, joyful, loving relationships. The negative scenarios described above do not imply that there are not many happy, loving families. In the midst of secular pressures, many families struggle successfully to maintain healthy, positive relationships. Nonetheless, today's crisis in family life challenges us to look seriously at our relationships and values.

The Church makes a tremendous contribution by challenging society to live by deep and authentic values, while drawing on the rich potential of modern technology. Jesus' teachings offer a powerful message for people desperately trying to make sense out of their fast-paced lives.

Catholics Are Changing

While waiting to catch a plane to Cincinnati, I waited in a bookstore at the San Francisco airport. Suddenly, I felt dizzy and held on to a table, lest I fall. Immediately, I noticed the table shaking, as items flew off the shelves onto the floor. It lasted for several seconds, and a clerk said, "Just another earthquake tremor."

At first, I was afraid, wondering what was happening. In contrast, the local inhabitants took it in stride and just kept working. I thought, "With a seismic shift going on, the locals act as if nothing is happening. Won't a 'big one' happen someday?"

This story illustrates what is going on in the Catholic culture today. Some recognize it, but many Church leaders go on as if nothing is occurring. Great religious cosmic shifts occur as the Catholic population shifts radically, witnessed by the changing population of American Catholics from the once bustling large city churches on the East Coast and upper Midwest to growing and developing parishes in the South and Southwest.

The age of the European immigrant is over, and their empty inner-city churches attest to it. This era is being replaced by a new wave of immigration from the Southern Hemisphere, Asia, Africa, and other countries, whose cultures are far different than that of Europeans. This is evidenced by the proliferation of Guadalupe statues and Hispanic celebrations in the Southwest and other areas of our country.

In addition, the other religious seismic shift involves what it means to be a Catholic and how to connect Catholic identity with a lifestyle far different from that of fifty years ago. Younger Catholics think nothing of claiming to be strong Catholics, while attending Mass infrequently. Such attitudes, developing from the grassroots, give far less credence to hierarchal structures and clerical authority than previous generations of Catholics did.

The reasons are multiple and complex, attributable in part to the Church's changing liturgical worship patterns that do not connect with many younger Catholics. In addition, the clergy sexual abuse scandal, and the bishops' response to it, negatively impacted the Catholic laity.

No simple answers exist to fix what has happened or to return to what is no more. *The new evangelization, however, will bear fruit to the extent that the whole Church — laity, clergy, consecrated religious, and pope — acknowledge the changing Catholic culture, embrace its positive elements, and start here in any efforts to reinvigorate the Church and share the Word of God in today's world.* To be successful, this new evangelization must acknowledge the changes in secular culture and the shifts in the Catholic culture. The latter includes the demographic changes that occur and the attitudinal shifts of Catholics on what it means to be Catholic in the twenty-first century.

3. Sectors of the New Evangelization

The *Lineamenta*, which prepared for the 2012 Synod of Bishops on the new evangelization, described various sectors operative in society in terms of attitudes, perspectives, or lenses through which we address life. In considering them, the *Lineamenta* indicated that it takes a hope-filled approach, requiring courage and the wisdom to read the signs of the times and know how to minister and witness.

The *Lineamenta* described five areas that require the Christian's special attention — cultural, social, communications, economic, and the civic and political sectors. The aim of the new evangelization is to bring the Gospel into all of them, thus influencing them and changing the outlook of the materialistic and relativistic attitude prevalent today.

Cultural Sector

Successful efforts at new evangelization require that parish leaders pay attention to cultural differences and shifts. These sensitivities will enable parishes to tailor their presentation of the Good News to the needs and situations of those they want to evangelize. Consider the following examples of cultural differences.

The culture of the Iroquois in New York differs from that of the Plains Indians in South Dakota. They are not the same, yet both live in the United States culture, inundated with technological advances and materialistic values. In the broader United States culture, both of these indigenous nations grow, mature, and form their attitudes toward life. Something similar is true in modern youth culture. While varying somewhat from place to place, the youth culture is remarkably similar because of television, the digital revolution, and instant communications.

Whatever the culture, the new evangelization must acknowledge and address it for the message of the Gospel to bear fruit (see *On the Permanent Validity of the Church's Missionary Mandate*, n. 37, c). In this regard, the multicultural nature of our parishes cannot be addressed by a "melting pot" mentality but rather by considering them as a mosaic of individual, yet united cultures.

With the increasing mobility of peoples, we experience the influx of various ethnic cultures, as they amalgamate with us. This is enriching and provides an occasion for growth, but often leads to corruption of traditional values, fluidity, lessening of ethnic traditions, and loss of cultural and personal identity. In one way or another, cultural assimilation affects the values and activities of social groups that formerly shared common interests, beliefs, and traditions.

Social Sector

With the increasing migration of peoples, significant social shifts are occurring in our country, especially in urban settings. Communities are being refocused before our eyes.

In rural areas of the United States, more and more people from South American countries are building new restaurants and forming a new workforce. As this happens, social-welfare systems are compelled to change their orientation. In urban areas, the same thing is occurring to a greater degree. In some parishes, once composed of Irish and German Catholics, we can now hear singing in Spanish, Vietnamese, or other languages. The mixing of cultures occurring in our communities now results in new forms of social responsibility, as well as crime, corruption, and violence.

The phenomenon of globalization is another aspect of the "new social sector." Globalization can be a vehicle to oppress the poor, but it also provides opportunities for increased solidarity among all peoples. This gives the Church an opportunity to see the new evangelization as going beyond local societies and regard it as a worldwide enterprise. As societies shift throughout the world, the new evangelization invites Catholics to recognize their mission as one of entering the new social sectors and transforming them in light of the Gospel, as well as to reach out to the poor, regardless of where they are.

Communications Sector

The media and digital culture is a powerful global force, changing the way people think, act, and respond. It affects every part of society, including the Church. The technology explosion is good for humankind, as long as it is a means helping humans be more human and to further God's kingdom, not serving as an occasion to suppress that kingdom, lessen moral values, and corrupt our children, as it spews out its messages of materialism, amorality, and relativism.

The new evangelization challenges Catholics to get more involved in the digital world and make a difference. It challenges pastors, consecrated religious men and women, pastoral ministers, and educators to help students discern the positive and negative impact of modern communications and to offer them ways to guard themselves against the unchristian values rampant in the media. Above all, it challenges parents to exercise wise discretion in helping their children sift through the rapidly changing digital world.

Economic Sector

The new evangelization challenges Christian business people to work for social justice and oppose movements that neglect the rights of workers and the corporate activities that minimize the equality between peoples, especially between our Northern and Southern Hemispheres. It also challenges consumers to put material wants and possessions in their proper place and to exercise charity in reaching out to the poor.

This is a formidable challenge, and one that pastoral leaders need to address in dealing with the needs of parishes. Parishioners need spiritual help in these matters, and the new evangelization offers pastoral ministers the opportunity to respond to their needs.

Civic and Political Sector

The new evangelization calls Christians to find new ways to strive for peace and equity among peoples. This means seeking fresh avenues for dialogue between rich and poor nations and among individuals. For Catholic politicians, it means acting morally and making political judgments in keeping with the norms of the Gospels and the teachings of the Church. It requires them to take the lead to help people live together in harmony and work for a better world.

4. Changing Culture — Media and Technology

Pastoral ministers can search for practical ways to enhance people's faith by using blogs, the Internet, and the social media. Brandon Vogt, in *The Church and New Media*, offers suggestions regarding what Pope Benedict XVI referred to as "embracing the digital continent."

We are in the midst of a technological revolution unlike anything before. The closest comparison is the invention of movable type in the West and the passage from an oral to a written culture over five hundred years ago. Learning how to navigate in the digital world, however, is not enough.

The new evangelization presumes a certain way of life, beginning with a commitment to Jesus. It's not sufficient to tweet or read articles about faith or to get new prayer forms on the Internet. That's fine in itself, but more is required. In the digital age, a great challenge is to foster a loving community of joy and hope in families and parishes.

The digital revolution cannot create a loving community. Only people can. This type of community begins with Christians who live and work in the digital world but go beyond it to connect their faith with joyful and painful life events. The new evangelization includes a growing realization that no matter what media we use, we must do more and proclaim Jesus' love to society, and use the media to foster Christian communities and invite people to grow.

5. The Parish in Contemporary Culture: The Challenge to the New Evangelization — Pastoral Reflections and Action Steps

The new evangelization invites pastoral leaders to think and act with energy, zeal, and hope. With this in mind, consider the following.

Pastoral Reflections

a. What do you think are the three biggest cultural challenges to the new evangelization in your town and parish?

b. In what ways is the culture of the Church changing? How do these changes affect your parish and its involvement in the new evangelization?

c. What is the cultural mix of membership in your parish? What impact do you think the diversity of backgrounds has on evangelization?

d. Which of the five sectors of the new evangelization is the biggest concern for your parish? Why? What strategy and tactics would you recommend to deal with its problems?

Action Steps

a. As a pastoral staff, review each of the five sectors mentioned in the *Lineamenta* for the synod and discuss it, asking what implications it has for your parish's evangelizing efforts.

b. Develop a plan to educate parishioners on contemporary culture and the new evangelization. Elements of the plan may include a speaker series during Lent, posting on the parish website articles or links to websites that deal with evangelization and culture, such as Father Robert Barron's WordOnFire.org.

c. Parish leaders should familiarize themselves with the impact of the digital revolution on evangelization. Consider studying together Brandon Vogt's *The Church and New Media*, including Matt Warner's chapter, "High-Tech Community: New Media in the Parish."

d. Parishes should identify several important but easy-to-implement ways of supporting families as they face the challenges of the changing culture. For example, work with the parish youth minister to develop a new awareness among teens regarding both the values and the dangers of social media.

Chapter Four

The New Evangelization and Ministry

This chapter is divided into five sections. To appreciate the new evangelization's role in carrying out the Lord's ministry, we begin by looking at Scripture in section one. The second section puts ministry in perspective and clarifies the term "ministry," as it relates to the new evangelization. Section three considers pitfalls to ministry, while section four analyzes evangelizing ministries. Finally section five offers pastoral reflections and action steps.

Ministry and evangelization are intimately related. They are a "both/ and," for one cannot exist without the other. Evangelization can be compared to the soul and ministry to the body. The soul (evangelization) is the energizing spirit of the body, whereas the body (ministry), composed of arms, legs, and other parts, enfleshes the soul and gives it life. Ministry puts flesh on Christ's command to teach all nations.

We begin with the story of Ellie.

Ellie, a parishioner, brought an elderly couple to Mass each Sunday. After seeing them for two years, I asked Ellie about her friends. I met them previously, but I didn't know the couple's background. Ellie said the man was Catholic, while his wife professed no religion.

The woman's sincerity impressed me, so I suggested that Ellie ask her if she ever thought about becoming a Catholic. Several weeks later, Ellie called me. She was overjoyed. When she spoke to her friend, the woman answered, "Thank you for asking. I've been waiting forty years for someone to invite me to be a Catholic."

Ellie's story illustrates the heart of the new evangelization — namely, inviting others through word and deed to share Jesus' message in a

Christian community. This can happen in families, parishes, among friends, and at work. When centered on God's kingdom, pastoral leaders carry on Jesus' work as reflected in the Scriptures. Just as Jesus' ministry fulfilled his mission, so Christian ministry carries out the Church's evangelizing mission. Seen in this way, evangelization is not a separate parish ministry, but central to all ministries.

The Good News of Jesus Christ bears little fruit unless we share it with others, for the ongoing incarnation of Jesus' message happens through us. This is an awe-inspiring task, requiring faith and humility. God calls us to communicate his message with parish and family members, friends, neighbors, and those who do not know Jesus.

This formidable task begins in the simplest ways — the love of a parent or friend, the sacrifice of a teacher or social worker, or the dedication of a parish leader. Evangelizing society requires a personal commitment and preparation on the part of those engaged in ministerial activities.

1. New Evangelization, Ministry, and Scripture

The new evangelization relies strongly on the wisdom gleaned from the Scriptures. As the *General Directory for Catechesis* says, "the Church desires that in the ministry of the word, Sacred Scripture should have a pre-eminent position" (n. 127). One of the most important tasks of Church ministry is to stress the significance of Scripture, for no real evangelization happens without the biblical message. These holy writings contain the earliest Christian witness to Jesus' life, teaching, and ministry.

The Gospel of Mark is the earliest narrative describing Jesus' call of the first apostles. Here, we read of Simon, Andrew, James, and John, who were seasoned fishermen (Mark 1:16-20). At Jesus' invitation, they followed him. What inspired them to leave families and work to respond to Jesus' calling and risk rejection and death?

Before inviting them to follow him, Jesus says, "The time is fulfilled . . ." (Mark 1:15; NRSV). The word that Mark used for "time" is *kairos*. This Greek word means quality time that is loaded with meaning, to distinguish it from *chronos* time, which is chronological or quantitative time. Mark's usage hints at why these men followed him. They saw in him the opportunity to become part of something really important, something with meaning. Initially, their *kairos* centered on a political messiah. They wanted to be a disciple of a man who would overcome the Roman occupation of Jerusalem and begin the messianic era foretold by the prophets.

Jesus' passion and death shattered their dream, but Pentecost enlightened them to their true calling to minister in *kairos* time. This mission was more important than earthly glory and power. Such a conviction moved them beyond the complacency of *chronos* time to the dynamism of *kairos* time, as they evangelized the world.

Jesus also invites parish ministers to live and minister in *kairos* time. This is difficult when society places heavy stress on events in *chronos* time. Here, we make money, build homes, develop computer programs, and live busy lives. In *chronos* time, it's easy to become complacent and mediocre, for such time never touches the deepest core of who we are. This happens in *kairos* time, or those moments when we experience love, like a mother's love when she sees her newborn child for the first time. It also occurs at beautiful weddings or funerals, or when a dedicated minister to the sick spends hours at the bedside of a dying person.

Parish ministers can learn a powerful lesson from Jesus' apostles, who never "got it" during his earthly life. Often, we do not get it either. We live week by week, year by year, giving lip service to our faith but never committing ourselves to our mission to evangelize. Such complacency happens in parish work and in families, where living in *chronos* time, caught up in the fast-paced, materialistic world is often the priority. For this reason, adults, youth, children, and parents, unable to find the *kairos* time they desire in the parish or at home, look elsewhere, sometimes turning to evangelical churches, or drowning their sorrows in alcohol, or engaging in questionable relationships.

Jesus invites us to examine our pastoral responsibility in light of *chronos* and *kairos* times. When *chronos* time predominates, little evangelical ministry may happen. Instead, we put our ministerial priorities in money, status, functional activities, meetings, and parish organizations. *Chronos* time canonizes maintenance. In ecclesial ministry, *kairos* time brings growth, energy, and life.

Reflecting on ecclesial ministry, we see how *chronos* time affects new evangelization efforts. Organization and management are necessary, but in themselves never inspire anyone to follow Christ. This happens in the flesh-and-blood witness of everyday life. In such witness, we fulfill our Christian mission.

Evangelization in one neighborhood illustrates *mission in action*. In this largely African-American area, ministry that happens there comes not only from the churches but also from the witness of Baptist shopkeepers and hairdressers.

In one establishment, Charisa, a middle-aged shop owner, put aside her work and said to a young woman, "Alicia, you look sad today." This began a prolonged conversation, culminating with Charisa asking Alicia, "Do you ever pray?" Alicia replied, "I don't know how to pray. Will you teach me?"

This initial contact led to more meetings in the store. One day Alicia joyfully told her mentor, "I am so happy. Next week I will be baptized in the Friendship Holiness Church." Because the shopkeeper gave Alicia *kairos* time, she heard God's Word. Charisa enfleshed her Christian mission in everyday actions. She set aside her daily work routine in *chronos* time to enter *kairos* time. Her actions remind us of Mark's words: "The time is fulfilled . . ." (Mark 1:15; NRSV).

The new evangelization in *kairos* time is the heart of pastoral ministry. Besides proclaiming the Good News of God's kingdom, Jesus invites us to continue this sort of ministry in our homes, neighborhoods, and parishes.

The new evangelization centers on fulfilling our mission in *kairos* time, a time pregnant with the power of the Holy Spirit. As the *General Directory for Catechesis* says, "evangelization must be viewed as the process by which the Church, moved by the Spirit, proclaims and spreads the Gospel throughout the entire world" (n. 48).

Just as Jesus fulfilled his mission through his life (being) and deeds (doing), so pastoral ministers accomplish their Christian mission by inviting others to share God's love in the Catholic Church. Here, individual and pastoral ministries converge.

2. Pastoral Ministry in Perspective

In a *wide* sense, "ministry" refers to individual or collective actions performed by Christians for the sake of the kingdom. These actions, carried out by Christian disciples, continue Jesus' ministry on earth. As with him, such flesh-and-blood witness is more powerful than words. *On the Permanent Validity of the Church's Missionary Mandate* (n. 42) says,

People today put more trust in witnesses than in teachers, in experience than in teaching, and in life and action than in theories. The witness of a Christian life is the first and irreplaceable form of mission: Christ, whose mission we continue, is the "witness" *par excellence* (Rv 1:5; 3:14) and the model of all Christian witness.

The term "ministry," used in this wide sense, is equivalent to *Christian service* or *discipleship.*

Recent Church documents restrict ministry to activities performed by Christians under the umbrella of the Church. In this *restricted* sense, it is limited to designated Church service or ecclesial ministry — for example, the work of an ordained priest, a pastoral associate, a catechist, or a religious education director. With this understanding, in *Called and Gifted for the Third Millennium* (p. 16), the U.S. bishops say,

> The lay faithful are engaged in ministries of other kinds that are also formative. They share the faith of the Church through teaching young people as well as adults; they serve in peace and justice networks, in soup kitchens and shelters, in marriage preparation, in bereavement programs, and in ministry to the separated and divorced. All these actions, when performed in the name of Jesus and enacted under the aegis of the Church, are forms of ministry.

Evangelization is the goal of all Christian ministry.

Ministry is rooted in our baptismal calling. As *Called and Gifted for the Third Millennium* (p. 15) says,

> Through the sacraments of baptism, confirmation, and eucharist every Christian is called to participate actively and co-responsibly in the Church's mission of salvation in the world. Moreover, in those same sacraments, the Holy Spirit pours out gifts which make it possible for every Christian man and woman to assume different ministries and forms of service that complement one another and are for the good of all (cf. *On the Vocation and the Mission of the Lay Faithful in the Church and in the World,* no. 20).

We are challenged to respond to our baptismal vocation by sharing the Good News of God's love. As the U.S. bishops say in the same document, "Everyone has a responsibility to answer the call to mission and to develop the gifts she or he has been given by sharing them in the family, the workplace, the civic community, and the parish or diocese" (p. 15).

Pastoral ministers use their gifts for God's glory and our neighbor's good. In our busy lives, we need to revitalize the Catholic custom, once widely practiced, of giving our whole day to God for Christian service through the Morning Offering. By our daily offering of family activities, work, parish service, and neighborhood outreach for the sake of the kingdom, we fulfill our Christian vocation.

All ecclesial ministry is linked in some way to the Church. Without this link, distortions happen, as evidenced in the following story.

A Catholic high school student told the principal that her religion teacher did not believe Jesus was God. This teacher said Jesus was a holy man, someone to follow. Upon questioning, the teacher admitted he did not believe Jesus was divine or really present in the Eucharist.

This teacher, once a strict Catholic, went through a rebellious phase, alienated himself from the Church, but still remained active in social causes. When what he was teaching became clear to school officials, he was treated fairly but replaced as a religion teacher.

He did not fulfill his responsibility as an ecclesial minister, for every Church minister is bound to be faithful to the beliefs and practices of the Catholic community.

3. Pitfalls to Ministry

The shifting ministerial focus in Catholic parishes brings with it a proliferation of ministries and more complex parish organizations. Two pitfalls exist regarding ministry and the new evangelization. The first pertains to parish ministry; the second to personal ministry.

The first pitfall occurs with the failure to have a clear ministerial focus and to link school ministry, catechesis or religious education, liturgy, social action, and other ministries. When a clear focus is lacking in parish ministry, parish activities can easily become compartmentalized and lead to turf building, competition, and politics, as well as duplicated efforts. In parishes lacking a unified vision, youth ministry often has little to do with religious formation or family ministry. Without a kingdom-centered vision, parish organization can be based more on a business model than on a ministerial one. Evangelization has limited success when parishes perpetuate politics and competition rather than Jesus' message of love, cooperation, and forgiveness.

Under the leadership of the pastor, the pastoral council and other parish organizations must work together to establish a clear focus, common vision, and solid direction for the parish's various ministries. An appreciation of evangelization, as the energizing center of all ministries directed to the kingdom of God, gives Church ministries this needed focus.

The second pitfall concerns personal ministry. It is due to failing to see work in the family and world as aspects of our call to Christian discipleship.

On the Vocation and the Mission of the Lay Faithful in the Church and the World says, "The *Christian family,* as the 'domestic Church,' also makes up a natural and fundamental school for formation in the faith: father and mother receive from the Sacrament of Matrimony the grace and the ministry of the Christian education of their children, before whom they bear witness and to whom they transmit both human and religious values" (n. 62, emphasis in original).

Often, the pope's message is missed by Catholics who fail to identify their service to family as an aspect of their Christian calling. The world, too, is not recognized by them as a fertile field to sow the Word of God. Many people do not see their everyday work as an opportunity for evangelization. For them, work is work and church is church. They do not link everyday life with church membership.

Mature Christians need to acknowledge their call from God to proclaim the kingdom. As *On the Vocation and the Mission of the Lay Faithful in the Church and the World* says, "*God calls me and sends me forth* as a laborer in his vineyard. He calls me and sends me forth to work for the coming of his Kingdom in history. This personal vocation and mission defines the dignity and the responsibility of each member of the lay faithful . . ." (n. 58, emphasis in original).

Fulfilling our call to proclaim the kingdom of God happens informally and formally. The *first* refers to activities that reflect Jesus' teaching without directly mentioning his name. Loving parents, business people who are just, and compassionate social workers evangelize informally. The *second* happens when people proclaim Jesus' message in catechesis, liturgy, sharing groups, or personal witness. Parents, teachers, homilists, and friends evangelize formally when they make explicit the message that Jesus and the Church teach.

To evangelize is to share faith. This faith sharing, also called *primary* or *core* evangelization, has several levels. First, a basic thrust of it is to nonbelievers, as the Christian community reaches out to "make disciples of all the nations" (Matthew 28:19; JB). Second, it is strongly oriented to unchurched, alienated, hurting, or disinterested people who may or may not have faith. Often they believe in Jesus but have problems with the Church. Third, faith sharing is directed to children, youth, or adults who are growing in faith. Evangelization deepens their belief in Jesus' message. Sharing faith is evangelization's constant call, inviting people to deeper levels of faith, dedication, and insight. Evangelization affirms that we have something which others seek and invites searchers to come and see.

4. Evangelizing Ministries

Evangelizing activity is the heart of pastoral ministry that has as its goal developing mature followers of Christ, willing to share their faith. The ministries of word, worship, and service are central aspects of these evangelizing efforts.

The *General Directory for Catechesis* says, "The ministry of the word* is a fundamental element of evangelization. The presence of Christianity amongst different human groups and its living witness must be explained and justified by the explicit proclamation of Jesus Christ the Lord" (n. 50).

This *ministry of the Word* happens in a parent teaching her child about God, a Catholic school religion class, parish catechetical sessions, adult religious programs, preaching, Scripture study groups, religious renewal

---

* Cf. Acts 6:4. The Ministry of the Word of God is fostered in the Church by:
— the ordained ministers (cf. CIC 756-757);
— members of institutes of consecrated life in light of their consecration to God (cf. CIC 758);
— the lay faithful in light of their baptism and confirmation (cf. CIC 759). In regard to the term *ministry (servitium)*, it is necessary that all reference be made to the uniqueness and to the source of all ministry which is the *ministry of Christ*. To a certain extent this applies also without ambiguity to the non-ordained faithful. In the original meaning, it expresses the work with which the members of the Church carry on the mission of Christ, both within the Church and throughout the world. However, when the term is distinguished from and compared with the various *munera and officia*, then it should be clearly noted that only in virtue of sacred ordination does the word obtain that full, univocal meaning that tradition has attributed to it (cf. John Paul II, Allocution at the Symposium on "The Participation of the Lay Faithful in the Priestly Ministry" n. 4, *L'Osservatore Romano*, English Edition, May 11, 1994 [emphasis in original].)

sessions, while evangelizing nonpracticing Catholics or inquirers, and in religious formation classes. Each helps people understand God's Word and apply it to life. The heart of these endeavors includes communicating the lived reality of the Paschal Mystery and encouraging Catholics to share their faith with others.

The *ministry of worship* celebrates the living Lord as central to life. The *General Directory for Catechesis* reminds us of the link between the Lord's presence in life and our celebration of this presence, when it says, "Christ is always present in his Church, especially in 'liturgical celebrations' (SC 7)" (n. 85).

In liturgy, we celebrate our joys and disappointments, as we join life events with Jesus' story. Baptism celebrates our rebirth as children of God, marriage celebrates our lives shared with a spouse and family, anointing of the sick celebrates the ongoing fulfillment of the Lord's promise to heal the sick, and the sacrament of the Eucharist celebrates Christ's real presence, as his eternal sacrifice renews us in word and sacrament.

During sacramental activities, the community gathers to honor God, celebrate oneness in faith, and welcome others. Few better times exist to show warmth and hospitality than on liturgical occasions such as Christmas, Easter, funerals, baptisms, and weddings. Then, kind words and warm hearts strengthen weak faith, nourish belief, reconcile alienated members, and invite nonbelievers to follow Jesus. Liturgy is a more powerful evangelizing activity than fish fries, bingos, festivals, and picnics, because vibrant liturgies help us celebrate God's special sacramental presence among us and appreciate how faith can make a difference.

The *ministry of service* includes pastoral activities like reaching out to the poor, helping the elderly, and consoling the sick. These are part and parcel of Christian evangelization. Our love, shown through service, inspires others to follow Jesus. As the *General Directory for Catechesis* states, "Evangelization . . . bears witness (EN 21 and 41; RM 42-43; AG 11) amongst peoples of the new way of being and living which characterizes Christians" (n. 48).

If we reach out in kindness, those served may ask, "What makes you tick?" "Why are you doing this for me?" or "What is your motivation?" As Christian evangelizers, we answer such questions by indicating how our Christian faith motivates our actions on behalf of charity and justice. We need to be bold in speaking about God, for such conversations help others appreciate Christ's message and the Church's ministry.

To link Church ministries with Jesus' call to evangelize, pastoral ministers encourage parishioners to follow the commandments, grow in deeper union with Christ and his mystical body, love their neighbors, practice the corporal works of mercy, reach out to those without faith, and welcome alienated Catholics and nonbelievers into the Christian community. In connecting modern evangelists with the past history of Catholic evangelization, *On the Permanent Validity of the Church's Missionary Mandate* says, "Today all Christians, the particular churches and the universal Church, are called to have the same courage that inspired the missionaries of the past, and the same readiness to listen to the voice of the Spirit" (n. 30).

5. The New Evangelization and Ministry: Pastoral Reflections and Action Steps

Pastoral ministers need to remind themselves of the essential role they play in furthering Jesus' kingdom on earth through their evangelizing efforts. The following questions invite them to reflect on the relationship between the new evangelization and ministry, and suggest action steps.

Pastoral Reflections

a. How does *kairos* time differ from *chronos* time? In what ways do you minister pastorally and personally in *chronos* and *kairos* times? What one thing could you do to increase your ministering in *kairos* time?

b. What are the connections between ministry and the new evangelization? What does this mean for the ways you conduct your personal and pastoral ministry?

c. What are some pitfalls of pastoral and personal ministry? How can they be avoided?

Action Steps

a. The parish should develop or refresh its vision and mission statements. The vision statement expresses in a sentence the overall goal of the parish community. The mission statement articulates the ways in which the parish community achieves the vision. Usually parishioners participate in the formulation of these statements along with the pastor and the parish staff. Consult your diocesan office for assistance in these efforts.

b. Establish a monthly one-hour meeting where pastoral leaders responsible for the ministries of word (education), worship (liturgy), and service (outreach) share plans and agree on ways of collaborating to assure a unified approach to evangelization.

c. Set aside fifteen minutes in staff meetings for pastoral leaders to evaluate their ministries in terms of *chronos* and *kairos* time. They can ask if they make room in the administrative aspects of their ministry for the Spirit to work in bringing others to Christ and the Church.

d. Conduct semi-annual evening or Saturday workshops designed to teach parishioners their responsibility for personal ministry in the family and at work, to show them how to begin and grow in it, and to motivate them to action.

Chapter Five

The New Evangelization and the Parish

This chapter adds further insights on pastoral ministry and the new evangelization. It is divided into five sections. The first section situates the parish in the wider Catholic community, while the second discusses key aspects of pastoral ministry. The third contrasts pastoral ministry in Catholic parishes with Protestant evangelical churches, and section four looks at evangelicalism, the new evangelization and Catholic parishes, and offers lessons to be learned. Finally, section five gives pastoral reflections and action steps to further the new evangelization.

The parish is central to the success of the new evangelization. It is the hub of Church life and the place to learn the Word of God and strengthen it through the vibrant witness of a loving Christian community.

We begin with the story of Kari.

While flying to New York, Kari, a business woman in her twenties, described to me how she found in an evangelical Protestant church what she missed in her Catholic parish. Kari spoke to me after noticing that I was reading a Catholic book. After asking if I was Catholic, Kari took out a Bible and referred to it as her "map of life."

She said,

> I grew up Catholic and attended Catholic schools and went to Sunday Mass. During these years, I never really connected with what was happening in the Church. Then, a colleague at work invited me to her Christian church. Here, I felt welcome and spiritually nourished. Not until I became a member of this evangelical

congregation did I appreciate the Bible as God's Word. Now, I live by it. It gives me knowledge and support.

This story challenges pastoral ministers to see their ministry in a positive way and to investigate ways of addressing the changing needs of Catholics. New ways of presenting Jesus' message are a significant emphasis in the new evangelization. To investigate these ways, we consider the parish.

1. Situating the Catholic Parish

The *Catechism of the Catholic Church* (n. 2179) quotes the 1983 Code of Canon Law, "A *parish* is a definite community of the Christian faithful established on a stable basis within a particular church" (CIC, can. 515 § 1, emphasis in original). This canon focuses a parish's orientation around a community base. Seen in this way, the parish is an established community of the Christian faithful that gathers on a regular basis to share faith in Jesus, to celebrate in liturgical worship, and to minister to God's people through works of charity.

A pastor leads a parish, which is part of a larger diocese. It teaches Jesus' message to parishioners and to the larger society, and it illuminates God's presence in life and worship. Great variety exists from parish to parish, but basic elements are the same.

2. Key Aspects of Pastoral Ministry

The parish performs many ministerial functions. Some notable ones include the following.

A. The Parish Roots Evangelizing Activities in Welcome and Hospitality

Effective parishes are welcoming parishes. Welcome is not only something people feel because a parish has greeters at Sunday Mass. Rather, real welcome permeates a parish's style, spirit, and vitality. It is an attitude that extends beyond Sunday Mass to parish clubs, organizations, and social gatherings. Such hospitality is apparent in the way secretaries answer the phone, custodians assist people seeking information, or the parish treats new parishioners.

An inhospitable attitude is not always obvious to established parish members. *"We've always done it this way"* or *"How dare a newcomer tell us what to do"* are slogans that turn people away from parish involvement. Some longtime parish members limit their involvement to their circle of family, friends, and acquaintances, while being insensitive to newcomers. The following episode from my father's life illustrates this point.

After my family joined a new parish, my dad attended an evening parish men's meeting alone. After walking from table to table, no one greeted him or asked his name. He felt isolated and unwelcome, while others chatted and had fun. After a short while, he left and went home. Dad never again went to another social there, although he remained a faithful parish member.

Sometimes, our state in life or ethnic background makes a difference in the welcome we receive. Many single people feel out of place at parish gatherings, organized around parents and children. African-Americans, Hispanics, Asians, and other ethnic groups may not feel welcome.

Parishes need to develop sensitivity to all peoples. This especially applies to members of other faiths on occasions like weddings, funerals, or graduations. Parishes should consider providing liturgical aides to help non-Catholics at such special times. Effective evangelization cannot happen without hospitality. It is central to Jesus' healing and forgiving ministry.

B. The Parish Gives People Support, in Addition to What They Receive From Their Family, Friends, Work, or Civic Associations

Often, it's hard to experience community, even among family and friends, due to changes in family life and our mobile society. Civic meetings, sports groups, fitness centers, and work environments connect us with people of similar interests, but these often do not satisfy our deeper need for community. We need a community experience that goes beyond superficial connections.

Parishes can provide opportunities for celebration, faith sharing, and ultimate meaning. They help us understand what is happening in our lives in light of Jesus' message. A parish needs to become a welcoming community. When people perceive the parish as just another organization, not meeting their ultimate needs, they may shy away from active membership. In such instances, Jesus' message is not heard because of the way these parishes communicate it.

A parish's success in evangelization does not depend on more organizational structures, finances, parish lists, or computers. In the *Pastoral Constitution on the Church in the Modern World*, Vatican II said that the modern parish stays in close contact with society. Today, it uses the media, the Internet, fax machines, organizational development, and business practices in ministry. Unfortunately, some parishes develop a bureaucratic style not significantly different from secular businesses. Although organization is necessary in parishes, they must keep their mission of proclaiming God's kingdom in the forefront. The following story may help parish ministers reexamine their priorities.

A pastoral council meeting was ready to begin, when the doorbell rang. A poorly dressed woman, trying to make ends meet in a difficult situation, asked to speak to a pastoral leader. Tears ran down her cheeks as she told her story. The leader, anxious to get to the meeting, gave her a few moments, excused herself, and asked the woman to return the next day. At the meeting, the council talked about helping the poor.

Later, the leader realized the irony of what had happened. The poor woman never came back. Parish ministers cannot respond immediately to every request, but exercising wisdom as concrete situations arise is vital. Few people show up at rectories or ministry centers unannounced. Perhaps such people get the impression that pastoral leaders are thinking, "Why are you bothering us? We've got work to do."

Parishes exist to live out the kingdom, not play politics, build bigger buildings, or arrange more meetings. Only in the context of God's kingdom does evangelization flourish.

C. A Parish Is Prophetic When the Prophetic Spirit Exists Within Its Organizational Structures

In the Judeo-Christian tradition, prophecy means *speaking for God*. It is rooted in community. God commissioned the Hebrews as a community to be prophetic through fidelity to the divine call. When they neglected this call, prophets like Isaiah, Ezekiel, and Jeremiah intervened and revealed God's designs for them. The prophets addressed people's particular circumstances in light of God's Word. Their voices challenged the established religious or social order when they were at variance with the designs of the Almighty.

Jesus opposed abusive civic and religious institutions in shaping his message of forgiveness, healing, and compassion. His prophetic mission exposed pharisaical religiosity by challenging them to return to the spirit of Judaism.

Prophecy exists in the parish when the risen Lord manifests his prophetic witness through the Christian assembly. His prophetic ministry proclaims Good News through the parish's evangelizing activities. Parishioners witness Jesus' presence by connecting their lives to the kingdom that Jesus proclaimed. The Christian witness in word or deed communicates God's prophetic Word.

A parish's organizational structure influences its vision of the Spirit's presence. It exercises powerful prophetic witness to Jesus' kingdom by modeling his compassion, healing, and forgiveness. Prophecy is incorporated into Church structures in two ways. The *first* brings the kingdom message into the institution itself. Here, parish ministers, associations, and volunteers live by a philosophy rooted in compassion, justice, forgiveness, and healing, reflected in the following story.

A sisters' community scheduled a conference at their motherhouse on a Sunday afternoon. Two sisters serving in a parish nearby prepared to leave for the gathering. While getting into their car, Jimmy, a neighborhood boy, approached them. His father died two months before. He told the sisters how hard it was at home and asked if they would come immediately to help his sick mother.

The sisters went with Jimmy and never made it to the conference. They chose people over meetings, incorporating the kingdom into their parish and community work. They could have said, "Sorry, Jimmy, we have to go to a sisters' conference, so we can't come now. We'll visit your home tomorrow." Later, the sisters explained to their community why they were not at the conference. Some people may not have been as compassionate as the sisters. Their action reflects the true spirit of the Gospel.

It's a challenge for parish ministers to incorporate the kingdom message into parish life. Some ways that this takes place include:

- Preferring people to meetings, structures, and activities.
- Paying a just wage to employees. Many parish employees, including ministers and Catholic schoolteachers, receive low wages. The excuse often given is that if people choose parish work, they cannot expect much of a salary. This argument is not

appropriate, for parish ministers also need money to live and raise a family.

- Putting priority on compassion, healing, and forgiveness. When parish leaders are symbols of reconciliation, their example evangelizes the entire parish.

The *second* way a parish incorporates the prophetic dimension is by challenging the community to practice justice and charity. In this regard, the parish distinguishes between justice and charity, illustrated in the following episode.

In a Midwestern city, gentrification of a poor neighborhood near the business district displaced the neighborhood's residents. After a poor, eighty-five-year-old man was found near death in an alley, the incensed residents raised cries of "We want justice, not charity." After reexamining the gentrification process, the civic leaders passed legislation to protect the poor.

A Catholic activist involved in the struggle said that her parish was the hardest group to convince. She said, "The parish gives money to the poor (charity), but when it comes to taking a stand for the poor (justice) and stepping on the toes of influential parish benefactors, the parish hesitates."

When such a response takes place, little prophetic witness or evangelization happens. Jesus spoke a message of justice. He never worried about keeping influential people happy. Parish leaders can learn from his example and encourage parishioners to become engaged in justice issues.

The effectiveness of the parish's prophetic challenge depends on how the parish lives out its calling. The United States bishops spoke out for economic justice in the words, "In a marketplace where too often the quarterly bottom line takes precedence over the rights of workers, we believe that the economy must serve people, not the other way around" (*Sharing Catholic Social Teaching: Challenges and Directions*, p. 5). In concrete terms, this message is proclaimed in the ways that a parish uses its prophetic voice to speak out for citizens' rights. A parish's stance on this matter is influenced by its ability to hear God's Word and communicate it.

A parish's ministry speaks eloquently about what the parish really believes. When parish ministry mirrors Jesus' compassion, justice, healing, and forgiveness, evangelization happens.

3. Catholic Parishes and Evangelical Churches

After a lecture on "Evangelicalism: Lessons for Catholic Evangelization" at a Religious Education Congress, many people remained, asking what to do about family members who joined evangelical churches. All their stories about teenage children leaving the Church were similar. Some parents cried, as they said,

> We are helpless. Our parish does little to encourage our youth in the Catholic faith. They feel unwelcome at Mass, because the liturgy does not speak to them. There are few religious or social activities to interest them in the parish. A nearby evangelical church welcomes them and provides meaningful Scripture studies. Our children go there. Some have joined this church.

Catholics of various ages join evangelical churches. The following story sheds light on why this sometimes happens.

I purchased some items at a local hardware store. Waiting to pay the bill, a man in line asked me, "Are you Father Hater?" After I answered in the affirmative, he said, "Do you remember me? I'm Jim Smith, a former student of yours."

I remembered him as a fine, dedicated college student. After a cordial exchange, he said, "I left the Catholic Church after I found the real church of Jesus Christ." He then identified the evangelical congregation that he now attends.

Jim said that he served Mass as a boy and participated in adult prayer groups. He continued, "I never found spiritual meaning in the Catholic Church. My parish offered few opportunities for me to grow in God's love. Now, I am fed spiritually in my new church."

We cannot conclude from the above story that many good things are not happening in Catholic parishes. Many Catholic congregations are welcoming communities, rooted in Gospel mission statements, and committed to Christian values. Through hard work, spiritual renewal, and ministry programs, they reach out to all ages and socio-economic groups.

Even when good things are happening in parishes, we cannot rest on these accomplishments. The needs of many Catholics are still not met, witnessed by those who leave the Church to join other churches. They challenge us to continually reexamine our ministry.

Catholic parishes need to listen to young people, including young adults, and get them involved in Church activities. This means inviting them to actively participate in the liturgy, ministry programs, pastoral council, and other parish functions. Young people look for opportunities to pray together, study Scripture, discuss their questions, and develop community. Peer pressure influences them to join friends who are engaged in the parish community. When parishes involve them in group activities, young people feel at home.

Various social and cultural factors influence Catholics to join evangelical churches. Cultural and family roots that nourished pre-Vatican II Catholics are not as evident today. Many Catholics under fifty often are unaware of *basic* Catholic teaching that their parents and grandparents learned. Likewise, strong family and social roots, giving previous generations a clearer identity, are not as evident.

Many Catholics are caught up in the pressure, relativism, and materialism of the times. They look for stability and meaning, but get few directions from secular society. Some find little security in their families, and less in parish communities. Beset with job pressures and challenges at home, they feel overwhelmed by daily responsibilities. Often their faith takes a back seat, for they never learned to appreciate the positive benefits that solid Catholic belief affords.

Society's superficial lifestyle does not satisfy them. Hence, they search for an anchor in this uncertain world. When their needs are not met in the Catholic Church, they may drop out, look elsewhere, or move into a personal spirituality devoid of church affiliation. Today's challenges cannot be met by the Church's return to a bygone era. Rather, parishes need to focus on core Catholic belief and practice in light of contemporary needs.

Today's changing family patterns and job pressures influence United States Catholics in subtle ways. Religious values are under stress as depersonalizing factors enter family life. These include social pressures for elementary school children to conform to the latest clothing fads, as well as sports activities that take children away from Sunday church services with their families. Unfortunately, some parents opt for a child's Sunday soccer game over Mass attendance. The implications of such a decision profoundly affect a child's attitudes and priorities. This decision is a hard one to make because of societal and peer pressures to participate in Sunday soccer games.

Cultural ambiguities leave people with a hollow feeling inside. They yearn for stability and a definite message that gives them direction. Some Catholics wish for a quieter time and connect with fundamentalist tendencies in the Catholic Church. Other Catholics without deep bonds to the Church join evangelical churches. Both groups point to needs that Catholic parishes have to consider in their evangelizing ministry.

Learn From the Evangelical Appeal

Evangelical churches proclaim a *simple message* — namely, *God loves you. Live by the Bible and you will be saved.* This message touches many people in our busy, complex world. Their fundamentalist interpretation of the Bible leaves little room for ambiguity, giving absolute answers in a complex world.

Evangelicals also stress a *personal message* of salvation, focusing on Jesus as Lord and Savior. This personal approach connects with the human quest for intimacy and holiness. It appeals to many sick, hurting individuals who lack significant human interaction. Belief in a personal bonding with Jesus is a powerful one. It hints at why TV preachers attract some Catholics who watch their programs. It also indicates why other Catholics attend evangelical churches that focus on Jesus as their Savior and Lord.

This personalistic orientation contrasts with the institutionalized structure of many mainline Protestant and Catholic churches. While institutionalization is necessary to ensure efficient parishes, it is critical that parishes focus on the simple, personal dimensions of faith. As parishes adapt to the needs of an increasingly complex world, they are challenged to keep in the forefront the core message of the Gospels, which stresses Jesus' love and forgiveness.

Evangelical churches send out a strong signal that they believe what they proclaim, witnessed by their *conviction and zeal.* A similar attitude is developing in Catholic parishes, among parishioners committed to the new evangelization. Such enthusiasm, often lacking in everyday life, impresses those searching for truths to believe. Evangelicals remind Catholics to be proud of what they believe by sharing it with others.

People search for *hospitable communities* in an impersonal world. Evangelical churches ground their ministry in hospitality. They welcome anyone to their assemblies, making visitors feel important. In a mobile society, reaching out to strangers is central to Catholic evangelizing ministry.

4. Lessons for Catholic Parishes

How would Catholic parishes change if they took seriously the lessons that spring from serious conversation with evangelicals? How do parishes provide a personal message, hospitality, community, stability, and certitude for Catholics? The following suggestions challenge Catholic parishes to evangelize their congregations and to invite others to join the Catholic community.

A. Catholic Parishes Need to Refocus All Ministry on the Kingdom of God, as Jesus Taught It

The Church exists to proclaim this kingdom, present wherever God is. Jesus taught us God's unique presence in poor, struggling humanity. This presence gives hope and a reason to endure suffering. God's kingdom offers life and freedom, desperately needed when we are broken and need forgiveness.

B. Catholic Parishes Are Challenged to Simplify and Personalize the Message They Proclaim

People had no difficulty understanding Jesus' teaching. They identified with his parables and understood his imagery of a Samaritan, a pearl, and the mustard seed. Such images touched their lives.

Jesus' teaching method offers important directions for homilists and catechists. Sophisticated theology or biblical exegesis do not inspire us — neither does talking over the heads of those being catechized. People want commonsense messages applicable to their experiences. Good homilies apply the biblical message to real life. Scripture comes alive when the Word of God connects with our stories.

Catechesis touches people's hearts when it connects with everyday life. As in preaching, catechists take into account those being catechized. The catechist helps them discover more about themselves in light of the kingdom and Church teaching. Catechesis also relates Christian belief to families and work. When parishes help us connect the Gospel message to life, we better understand how daily life is where we work out our eternal salvation.

Evangelicals teach a definite message. Catholic catechists, likewise, need to emphasize the basics of the Catholic faith. Otherwise, their teaching is incomplete.

C. Catholic Parishes Have to Underpin All Parish Activities and Ministries With Community and Hospitality

The Gospels portray all sorts of people seeking out Jesus. They sensed that he was someone special. When feeding the multitudes, we witness his compassion and desire to make the crowds feel welcome (John 6:1-15). Today, people need to feel welcome at parish functions, especially the Eucharist. As we have seen, the responsibility for parish hospitality extends to all parishioners. Parishes are challenged to develop a *welcoming spirit* that permeates the entire community, beginning in Catholic families and extending to parish and neighborhood affairs.

Christian community happens when two or more people share the kingdom message on a regular basis. A parish cannot decide functionally at a meeting how to create community. Community develops as people gather in faith, centering their life and ministry on the risen Lord. The Spirit of the living God provides the energy, joining parishioners in the Body of Christ. When Christians gather as God's people and commit themselves to love, justice, and forgiveness, community comes alive.

D. Catholic Parishes Need to Reflect the Pride and Zeal That Inspires Parishioners and Carries Over Into Their Homes and Work

Such enthusiasm invites us to take seriously our call to evangelize. It helps us to do good, avoid evil, and gives us confidence in an uncertain world. It is a key to establish Catholic identity and to inspire Catholics to be kingdom people. It enables us to appreciate our responsibility to evangelize in Jesus' name.

As we identify with Jesus' message, enthusiasm helps faith grow. As *Thy Kingdom Come* says, "The enthusiastic embrace of Catholicism is the way to grow in intimate love of Jesus Christ, to be personally converted to him, and to follow him as faithful disciples" (p. 2). Catholic pride begins in families. If parents criticize parish, school, clergy, and pastoral ministers, they send a negative message to their children. If they are away frequently from their families at parish activities, children may see the parish as robbing them of parental time. This does not imply that parents should avoid being honest about parish strengths and weaknesses, or that they should drop out of all parish activities. It does mean, however, that positive, constructive attitudes are necessary to help family members regard the parish as an important aspect of their lives. It also means that parents need prudence when deciding how much time to spend in parish ministry.

Positive attitudes encourage children, youth, and adults. When this happens, zeal and enthusiasm carry over to friends, neighbors, work associates, and parishes. Then, it's easy to be proud of being a Catholic.

E. Catholic Parishes Are Challenged to Emphasize the Basics of the Faith

Each parish is entrusted with teaching parishioners the fundamentals of the faith. Flexibility is the norm, as parishes develop various ways to serve parishioners. For some parishes, this means new opportunities for people to study Scripture, pray, and learn the Church's teaching. The *Catechism of the Catholic Church* and publications based on it are excellent sources for teaching the fundamentals of Catholic belief and practice.

Catechesis, especially adult catechesis, must be a top ministerial priority. Today, many people under fifty have fuzzy knowledge of basic Catholic beliefs. The situation is improving with increased emphasis on Catholic belief by catechists. Ignorance in younger years often makes it harder for Catholics to accept Church teachings as they grow older.

Parishes need to concentrate on teaching the basics of Catholicism. These include Scripture, sin, grace, the sacraments, morality, Jesus, and the Church, as well as helping people appreciate the Eucharist, sacramental life, the liturgical year, the Rosary, devotions, and personal and family prayer.

F. Catholic Parishes Need to Put a High Priority on Lay Leadership in Ministry

When lay people assume ownership of parish ministries, new energy pulsates through parish life.

Such ownership is necessary with the declining numbers of priests and religious men and women. Presently, lay people serve in parish leadership positions, and parish stability increasingly rests with the parish community. The pastor cannot be the main focus of a parish's identity. With the limited tenure of pastors, it's important to center parish stability in the people. This enhances a new *Catholic spirit* in parish life.

G. Catholic Parishes Are to Foster a Deep Love for Scripture

Evangelicals can show Catholic parishes the power that the Scriptures have in our lives. Since the New Testament came from the early Christian Tradition, it's time to recapture its significance in evangelizing efforts. Studying and praying with Scripture helps us fill spiritual gaps, as we face concrete realities of secular life.

Biblically-Based Pastoral Efforts

Catholic pastoral leaders exercise biblical wisdom when basing their ministerial efforts on love for Scripture. No reason should exist for Catholics to leave their parish and join another church to discover Jesus as their personal Savior and to learn his biblical teachings.

The way Catholic parishes form biblically based communities, centered on the kingdom of God, varies from place to place. Whatever direction it takes, the following are important components:

- Love for and knowledge of Scripture on the part of the pastor and ministerial team.
- Opportunities for parishioners to study Scripture and pray with it in parish settings and in their homes.
- A resource center with Bibles, commentaries, books, and tapes about Scripture for borrow or purchase.
- Commitment to begin each parish project, meeting, or session with Scripture.
- Opportunities for children's and youth catechists to learn Scripture.
- Sessions for parents, instructing them on how to teach Scripture to their children.
- Retreats and days of renewal based on Scripture.
- Catechetical sessions for children, youth, and adults, including children in Catholic schools, stressing the centrality of Scripture.
- A parish style that relates service functions to Scripture (for example, reading from the Bible before a St. Vincent de Paul Meeting), where a participant reads a Bible passage and discusses how Jesus' words and deeds relate to the group's ministerial activities.
- Homilies centered on applying Scripture to everyday life.

The new evangelization challenges parishes to examine their spirit, style, and organizational structures to see if they give people's needs sufficient consideration. This may require reviewing a parish's mission statement and planning process, and giving top priority to solid teaching, good liturgies, and service activities.

The new evangelization does not necessarily ask Catholic parishes to do more by way of programs and activities. The real challenge is to be a more welcoming, healing, and evangelizing parish, inspired by faith and knowledge of Catholic beliefs and practices.

5. The New Evangelization and the Parish: Pastoral Reflections and Action Steps

The new evangelization is associated with ongoing parish-renewal efforts. Based on the insights gleaned from this chapter, consider the following pastoral reflections and action steps.

Pastoral Reflections

a. Why do many Catholics leave the Church to join evangelical churches? What is it about evangelicalism that appeals to them?

b. Why are hospitality and community important for a parish's approach to the new evangelization?

c. What are the ways a parish can incorporate a prophetic spirit into its organizational structures?

d. What do you think your parish could learn from evangelical churches?

Action Steps

The chapter lists seven lessons from evangelicalism that parishes should take into account as they shape their ministries for the new evangelization. The pastoral staff should consider the implications of each for the parish and decide on easy-to-implement but important action steps to improve parish ministry. These might include the decision to:

a. Refocus all ministries on the kingdom of God.

b. Simplify and personalize the message these ministries proclaim.

c. Build community and hospitality into all ministries.

d. Serve with pride, zeal, and enthusiasm.

e. Emphasize the basics of the faith.

f. Put a high priority on lay leadership in ministry.

g. Foster a deep love for Scripture.

Chapter Six

The New Evangelization and the Ministries of Word, Worship, and Service

All evangelization centers around Jesus Christ and his message, which is taught, celebrated, and lived. This chapter addresses the chief ministries where this happens in four sections. Section one talks about the ministry of the Word, while the second looks at the ministry of worship. Section three analyzes the ministry of service. These three interrelate as part of a unified whole, energized by the new evangelization. Section four offers pastoral reflections and actions steps.

We begin with the story of three children.

A young girl and two boys sat in the front church pew each Sunday. No adult came with them. Lisa was about nine; her brothers were six and four. Their poor clothes suggested that they came from a struggling family. As the months progressed, I saw them more often in the school-yard. The girl helped at bingo. Their parents were divorced, and the children lived with their grandmother. Lisa, the oldest child, received Communion each Sunday.

The week before Catechetical Sunday, I announced that the religion class sign-up for children attending public schools was to be in the church vestibule after Mass. Parents were to make the necessary arrangements. During the recessional after Mass, as I walked down the aisle, the poorly dressed children followed me. When I got to the vestibule, Lisa, looking at me, blurted out anxiously, "Father, who will teach us about God?"

Who will teach us about God? These words reflect the challenge of the new evangelization. I sensed God's presence with Lisa and her brothers.

In their simple way, they reflected Jesus' message of love. Lisa taught her brothers about Jesus (word), celebrated God's presence with them at Mass (worship), and supported them (service). She was a remarkable nine-year-old girl.

This story invites pastoral ministers to focus on Jesus, who proclaimed a kingdom of love. All Church ministries further the ongoing communication of God's love. This love is shared, as Jesus' dying and rising continues. Evangelization witnesses in word and deed Christ's incarnate love. Through the Christian community, the risen Christ invites us to follow him as evangelizers.

All Christians share in Jesus' mission of furthering God's kingdom. This mission has three aspects: to proclaim and teach God's Word, to celebrate the sacred mysteries, and to serve the people of the world. Although we discuss these aspects separately, they cannot exist in isolation, even though in a particular ministry, or at a given time or place, one or the other predominates. Each includes the others, as pastoral ministers evangelize in light of the Paschal Mystery, the energizing center of evangelization.

When we proclaim the dying and rising of Jesus, evangelization energizes our endeavors, thereby reminding us of our mission to hasten God's kingdom. As the *General Directory for Catechesis* says, "evangelization must be viewed as the process by which the Church, moved by the Spirit, proclaims and spreads the Gospel throughout the entire world" (n. 48). Without it, various pastoral ministries designated to proclaim the Gospel, to celebrate it, or to serve others lack the dynamism promised by the Good News.

The new evangelization in a community of word, worship, and service constitutes the heart of the Church's witness. As an ongoing activity of the parish, effective evangelization requires a healthy balance among these three ministries.

1. Proclaiming the Word of God

God's Word comes to us in many ways. Rooted in Jesus' revelation and assisted by God's grace, we proclaim God's Word as Christian disciples. Such a response needs constant deepening, as we journey to God. This journey invites us to evangelize others along the way.

Christianity is Good News. To appreciate this message means discovering the power of God's Word in our lives. John's Gospel begins,

"In the beginning was the Word: and the Word was with God and the Word was God" (John 1:1; JB). John then describes the unfolding of God's revelation, centered in the Word.

The creation of the world began a process of God's self-communication with creation, climaxed in Jesus, and continued in the Church. The parish proclaims the Word-made-flesh sacramentally and through ministries that reflect God's plan of salvation. As the *General Directory for Catechesis* says, "The ministry of the word, within the context of evangelization, transmits Revelation, through the Church, by using human words" (n. 50).

The *ministry of the Word*, in a pastoral context, takes various forms. The *General Directory for Catechesis* describes them as "the first announcement or missionary preaching, pre- and post-baptismal catechesis, the liturgical forms and the theological forms" (n. 52). Pastoral ministers need to give special consideration to the liturgical form of preaching and the catechetical forms.

Preaching the Word

Referring to the homily as a ministry of the Word, the *General Directory for Catechesis* says, "It [the ministry of the word] takes different forms but amongst them the most important is the homily" (n. 51). Then, the document continues, "At this table of the word of God, the homily occupies a privileged position, since it 'takes up again the journey of faith put forward by catechesis and brings it to its natural fulfillment, at the same time it encourages the Lord's disciples to begin anew each day their spiritual journey in truth, adoration and thanksgiving' (cf. CT 48; cf. SC 52; DV 24; DCG [1971] 17; *Missale Romanum, Ordo Lectionum Missae,* n. 24 Editio Typica Altera, Libreria Editrice Vaticana 1981)" (n. 70).

Effective preaching is a powerful gift to the Christian community. Priests and deacons who proclaim God's Word by connecting it to our everyday joys and struggles affirm us in our Christian life. Unfortunately, some parishioners do not receive support, insight, and wisdom from Catholic preaching, if the preaching is over their heads or does not relate to their lives. A sign of this dissatisfaction may be the movement away from the Catholic Church by people who drop out of the Church entirely or join other churches.

The readings at Mass focus on God's dealing with the Israelites in the Hebrew Scriptures and on Jesus' life and teaching in the Christian

Scriptures. These words, written in a different cultural context, contain core messages applicable to every historical time. The homilist has to connect this core message to our present circumstances. The priest or deacon is challenged to address us in the context of our families, jobs, and social life, aiming to inspire us to become more faithful followers of Jesus. Preachers gain valuable help by identifying our needs, hopes, and struggles. Then, as the homilist proclaims God's Word, the Scriptures connect with what is happening in our lives.

For Catholics in church at Sunday Mass, the homily is a spiritual lifeline, intended to help them appreciate how God's Word touches daily activities. Every homilist, even if not a charismatic preacher, needs to proclaim the Word of God in a prayerful, simple way. Preaching is not an exegetical session where the latest in biblical scholarship is presented. Effective preaching relates Scripture to life.

The connection between catechesis and liturgy is vitally important. In liturgical celebrations, we worship God, reflect on the Word, experience the living Lord, and receive Jesus in the Eucharist. Our faith deepens and grows as a result of participating in the liturgy. As we do so, we hunger to know more and to share what we have learned with others through evangelization, catechesis, and witness.

Effective Catechesis

The journey of faith is lifelong. So is the need to hear God's Word again and again. This continued proclamation of the Good News is a central responsibility of pastors and parish catechists, who play a vital role in the new evangelization.

Catechesis is closely linked with a person's ongoing need for conversion, which begins in childhood and lasts until death. The *Rite of Christian Initiation of Adults* emphasizes that coming to faith and growing in faith involves questioning, learning the Good News, appreciating membership in the Christian community, and deepening our yes to Christ and the Church (RCIA, n. 1ff.).

As a ministry of the Word, "the definitive aim of catechesis is to put people not only in touch but in communion, in intimacy, with Jesus Christ" (*On Catechesis in Our Time* [CT], n. 5). Catechesis assists Church ministries in their attempts "to make disciples, to help people to believe that Jesus is the Son of God, so that believing they might have life in His name (cf. Jn 20:31), and to educate and instruct them in this life and thus build up the Body of Christ" (CT, n. 1). As one element in the evangelization process (CT, n. 18), catechesis has the same content as evangelization — namely, Jesus and his Gospel.

Pastoral ministers need to recognize that the Word of God is at the heart of all evangelizing activities. Consequently, the Catholic community places top priority on the Scriptures. This is especially important in family and youth ministries.

Some parents, discussing why their children know so little about the faith, excuse themselves by saying something like, "We do not know how to teach our children. We learned little about our faith while growing up." Acknowledging the theological illiteracy of such parents, parishes can look at ways to evangelize and instruct parents in Scripture and Church teaching.

Some parishes establish intergenerational catechetical programs, where parents are catechized along with their children. Here, after parents are instructed, they in turn catechize their children. Parishes who use this approach can provide an environment where parents learn to appreciate their faith and bring it into their homes.

Other parishes establish different approaches to faith formation and catechesis for children, youth, and adults. Often, the approach selected depends on the size and location of the parish, as well as the orientation of the pastor and parish staff. Regardless of which approach is used, family ministry is at the heart of the new evangelization, and family catechesis needs to be a top parish priority.

It is also important to provide opportunities for young people to learn the Word of God. Many young people have not made a commitment to any church. In their search for God, however, they are attracted to God's Word, revealed in Scripture. Pastoral ministers are encouraged to form Catholic Youth Evangelization Teams, centered in Scripture and dedicated to personal faith development and peer faith-sharing.

Systematic Catechesis

Catechesis happens informally, when a mother or father teaches a child about God, or when a college campus minister discusses how faith can make a difference in the life of a student. Such catechesis creates a positive climate for more systematic hearing of God's Word in parish liturgy or catechetical sessions. Systematic catechesis presents the entirety of the Catholic belief and practice in an orderly and sequential way. It can take place in parish catechetical sessions, Catholic-school religion classes, and a variety of other places. The pastor and other catechetical ministers are responsible for seeing that this happens. It requires preparation and an overall plan, where participants learn the basics of the Catholic faith.

Blessed John Paul II describes systematic catechesis as a "matter of giving growth, at the level of knowledge and in life, to the seed of faith sown by the Holy Spirit with the initial proclamation and effectively transmitted by Baptism" (CT, n. 20). He also says that systematic catechesis has "the twofold objective of maturing the initial faith and of educating the true disciple of Christ by means of a deeper and more systematic knowledge of the person and the message of our Lord Jesus Christ" (CT, n. 19).

How to Catechize

Catechesis can take different forms. It always begins with an initiative from God to share the Good News and involves a response of the Christian community to God's invitation. Sometimes, the generic expression "catechetical process" is used to help catechists devise effective ways to catechize. This expression can refer to different methods of doing catechesis. The most effective method often depends on the culture, climate, gifts, and skills of the catechists. In dealing with adolescents, versed in the use of computers and the Internet, the catechetical process can employ technological tools to connect with their need for acceptance, identity, and support.

Effective catechesis includes the following components.

A. Proclaiming Clearly and Accurately the Biblical Message or Basic Teaching of the Church

The most basic way to ensure good catechesis is to have well-prepared catechists. A catechist needs to be a person of faith, know the teachings of the Church, and have a good foundation in Sacred Scripture and the living Tradition of the Church.

The catechist presents the basic teaching or belief in a clear and accurate way and then applies it to the lives of those being catechized. When done effectively, the message taught both informs and forms those being catechized.

Many catechists have only a very basic knowledge of what they teach. When this is the case, those responsible for catechists need to help catechists identify the basic teachings of the faith and to use effective means to convey them. It is advisable that the basic beliefs to be taught are conveyed clearly to catechists, prior to the catechetical session, and that catechists are helped to devise effective ways to convey them.

B. Taking Into Account the Experience or Situation of the Person or the Group to be Catechized

To catechize effectively, what is taught must be connected with the experience of the one being catechized. St. Matthew did this in his Gospel, intended primarily for Jews and converts from Judaism. To relate to them, he often used Old Testament passages to show how Jesus fulfilled the prophecies about the coming Messiah.

In a similar manner, today's catechists need to show how the message being taught connects with the real-life situations of those being catechized. In this regard, the catechist can remember the words of the *General Directory for Catechesis*. It says that human experience "arouses in man, interests, questions, hopes, anxieties, reflections and judgments which all converge to form a certain desire to transform his existence." When a catechist taps into a person's experience, this "promotes the intelligibility of the Christian message" (n. 152). Hence, the catechist is challenged to illuminate the faith of those catechized.

The *General Directory for Catechesis* emphasizes that many methods can successfully present the Catholic message, including inductive and deductive ones (n. 150). Through stories, lectures, intellectual explanations, dramas, audiovisuals, the Internet, digital technology, social media, and discussions, the method that a catechist employs helps those catechized to appreciate the depth and beauty of Catholic belief. It is wise to use various ways to catechize, for no single one touches all people.

C. Using the Necessary Means to Help Those Catechized to Understand, Reflect On, Assimilate, and Make One's Own the Material Taught

The catechist invites and sometimes challenges those being catechized to make the message taught a part of themselves and to see how it can make a difference in life. This integration of message and life involves reflection and prayer. *Making the message one's own* is a central component of catechesis. In so doing, the person being catechized recognizes that what the catechist is teaching can change one's life.

D. Encouraging Those Being Catechized to Respond to the Message in Acts of Prayer, Liturgy, and Service to God's People

Growing in faith always means accepting God's invitation to change. When our faith grows, we change. This requires a personal response and leads to more intense social involvement, greater concern for family members, and commitment to live by Christian ethical norms in business and personal life. It may mean changing certain practices or adopting new ones. It also leads to deeper prayer and liturgical life.

Whatever catechetical approach is used must be faithful to the Scriptures, Church teaching, Tradition, and personal experience. This happens most effectively in community, where God is disclosed through the Church's faith. Effective catechesis continually invites us to probe more deeply into God's love in our everyday lives. As Blessed John Paul II says in *On Catechesis in Our Time*, "catechesis is necessary both for the maturation of the faith of Christians and for their witness in the world" (n. 25).

Adult Catechesis

Pastoral ministers need to focus on the three forms that adult catechesis takes. Each relates to an important dimension of adult life. These are the adult as an adult; the adult as a parent, spouse, child, or friend; and the adult in wider society, including the workplace.

First: *The adult as an adult.* Adults need supportive ministry. If they do not grow spiritually as people, other responsibilities often suffer. For this reason, adult catechesis examines issues like identity, well-being, solitude, affirmation, growing old, sickness, and leisure. Adult catechesis centers on relational and personal needs. To proclaim the Good News of God's love, people need support from a believing community.

Second: *The adult as a parent, spouse, child, or friend.* Such roles bring unique obligations and needs. Parenting is a complex vocation with many challenges, including teaching children to love God and neighbor. Often, parental responsibilities and work outside of the home tax spousal love. Effective preaching and catechesis acknowledges this reality in trying to help spouses grow in their love of each other.

Many adults are called upon to care for aging parents. Catechesis should help them see such responsibilities as privileges, not burdens. Adults also need friends beyond their immediate family. Catechesis should help them model such friendships after the friendship of Jesus with Mary Magdalene, John, and the other disciples.

Third: The adult in wider society, including the workplace. Adult catechesis must be sensitive to demands made upon adults in the workplace. They need help dealing with work issues that influence personal and family life. Take the example of Alicia, a young woman who spoke sadly about her mother. She said, "It's too late for my mother and me. All through my childhood and adolescence, I wanted her to attend my school plays, dance lessons, and athletic events. She was too busy on the fast track, advancing up the corporate ladder. My mother compensated by giving me anything I wanted. Her gifts soon grew stale. The things she gave me turned me against her when I realized that the one thing I wanted, she refused to give me. I wanted her time, which she jealously kept to herself, giving it instead to her work. Nothing she does now can recapture those lost years. I'll never have the intimacy with her that I intend to give my children."

Evangelization, centered in catechesis and preaching, should help adults see the importance of balancing their family and professional responsibilities.

Adult catechesis must also show people the right path to take in sharing Jesus' Good News in activities beyond their home. It must take into account how sharing Jesus' message relates to interactions of adults in their workplace, neighborhood, and social and civic affairs.

Regardless of its form, adult faith formation centers on the ongoing process of bringing us to deeper holiness and commitment to Jesus Christ. As *Our Hearts Were Burning Within Us: A Pastoral Plan for Adult Faith Formation in the United States* says, "As its first goal, faith formation helps adults 'to acquire an attitude of *conversion to the Lord*' (*Adult Catechesis in the Christian Community*, no. 36). This attitude fosters a baptismal spirituality for adults" (p. 23, emphasis in original). In addition, as this document explains, adult catechesis encourages us to grow in relationship with our parish community. This involvement keeps our faith active and growing in conjunction with other adult believers. As we grow in our relationship with the Lord in a community of Christians, we see more clearly our call to discipleship, moving us to evangelize those around us, at home, in the neighborhood, the workplace, and the world (p. 24).

2. Celebrating Faith through Worship

The Christian is never content with hearing the Word alone. God's call leads us to gratitude, thanksgiving, and the nourishment of our faith. We celebrate faith in liturgical ministry, the major responsibility for which belongs to priests, deacons, and liturgical ministers.

Christians come together in the liturgy to thank and praise God, who died for our sins and invites us to share our faith in Jesus' resurrection. Christian life is a marvelous act of praise, brought to fruition as we, united by God's Word and sacrament, say "Amen" over and over again to Jesus' abiding presence with us. As the *General Directory for Catechesis* says, "Communion with Jesus Christ leads to the celebration of his salvific presence in the sacraments, especially in the Eucharist" (n. 85).

The *ministry of worship*, the second focal point in the evangelization process, includes liturgy and prayer. Christian worship praises God and celebrates our redemption from sin and death. It celebrates the values from which our faith springs.

The *Rite of Christian Initiation of Adults* ritualizes the dynamics inherent in our Christian journey toward the kingdom. It is a significant aspect of the new evangelization in that it initiates people more deeply into the mystery of Jesus' dying and rising within a faith community. It presupposes that, on their faith journey, people are on different faith levels and need the support of a Christian community to maximize their call to discipleship.

The Church relates evangelical activity to the conversion process, which discloses three parish responsibilities. The *first* is responsibility to active Church members. Because conversion is lifelong, we grow together through catechesis, worship, and service. The *second* directs ecclesial ministry toward baptized Christians who do not know or hardly appreciate God and the Church. The parish community invites them to learn the Good News. The *third* initiates non-baptized people into the Church. The community helps them discover whether the Lord is inviting them to follow him by becoming active Church members.

Evangelization and conversion, centered on the Paschal Mystery, are integral aspects of our coming to faith. Conversion includes individual and ecclesial elements, taking into account our intellectual, moral, and religious growth. The RCIA, in ritualizing ongoing conversion, celebrates a person hearing God's Word and responding in Christian service.

All liturgical activities have a catechetical component. Referring to the connection between liturgy and catechesis, the *General Directory for Catechesis* quotes *On Catechesis in Our Times*, which states, "Catechesis is intrinsically bound to every liturgical and sacramental action" (n. 30).

All liturgy centers on the Eucharist, which plays a vital role in coming to faith and growing in faith. Although it is the center and summit of the Christian life, many Catholics fail to understand its meaning.

Some Catholics do not appreciate Christ's real presence in the Eucharist. This is evident when dealing with undergraduate and graduate theology students. In spite of their previous Catholic education, many do not understand Catholic Eucharistic beliefs. They know something about the ritual itself, but why Catholics celebrate it and what it really means are often unknown.

Many Catholics do not appreciate the Eucharist as a great prayer of praise and thanksgiving. This ignorance leads to an individualistic attitude, culminated in skipping Mass, because *they don't get anything out of it*. They fail to connect the Eucharist, Last Supper, and Jesus' death and resurrection. They do not know that the principal priest at every Eucharist is Jesus, who brings the memorial of Christ's unbloody sacrifice on the cross to our altars every time the Mass is celebrated. They do not know that God is present in the assembly of the faithful, the priest-presider, the Word proclaimed, the Eucharist celebrated, and the sacred consecrated species. They do not know how to connect Jesus' sacrifice on the cross with sacrifices they are called to make to be faithful disciples. In short, they do not understand the basics of the Mass.

The new evangelization places high priority on teaching Catholics to understand the Eucharist. Such understanding opens up new avenues of faith and dispels the ignorance leading to skepticism and disbelief. Catholics need to know how Jesus' *real presence* in the Eucharist connects with his presence throughout life. This is especially important for our youth.

The Eucharist is at the heart of the new evangelization. It complements the strong stress in Catholic evangelization on the ministry of the Word, especially Scripture. Evangelization falls short without a strong Eucharistic component. Hence, Catholic evangelization efforts center on the Eucharist as the summit toward which other evangelical activities tend.

If a person truly believes that the Word, who created the universe and every human being, is the same Word that dwells in the Eucharist, would the individual neglect receiving our Lord or consider the Eucharist as unimportant? The new evangelization reminds us that when we receive Communion, we take into our bodies the Lord of the universe, who made us and will judge us at the end of life. In unity with our Eucharistic Lord, our eternity has already begun.

What better way to evangelize, Catholic style, than to help people see this great mystery of our faith! When people believe it, they no longer take the Eucharist lightly. Then, the Eucharist itself evangelizes.

3. Serving the Needs of the Community and the World

When I was a boy, an old black man named Ezra pushed a small cart up Poplar Street, adjacent to our family store. With bent back and sparkling eyes, he cried out, "Rags, old iron!" as he struggled slowly up the street. In the summer, he sold ice for peoples' iceboxes and bought old rags and pieces of scrap iron.

As he pushed his cart, children often danced around him, asking for a piece of ice to cool the summer's heat. Responding to their requests, Ezra took his ice pick, cracked off pieces of ice, gave them to the children, and told his little friends to be good.

In the winter, he replaced the ice with coal. His chant became "Coal, coal!" as he sold small blocks of coal to heat homes in this poor area. When he got tired, he often entered our store and sat with my dad. I never spoke to him, but I admired his goodness and smile.

Each year at Christmas, Ezra came into our store and poured out a bag of coins on the counter. He always said, "Mr. Hater, will you count it? How much can I buy this year?" Then, Dad told him to pick out what he needed. Before I got wise, I wondered why Dad always told Ezra that he had just enough money for whatever items he put on the counter.

One year, I thought, "How can those few coins pay for all that merchandise?" His choice of merchandise always baffled me. Each year, he selected children's shoes, blouses, dresses, socks, underwear, pants, shirts, and toys. After Dad and Ezra concluded their business, they talked and wished each other a Merry Christmas.

When in high school, I asked Dad about Ezra. "He is a wonderful old man, Bob," Dad said. I replied, "He sure must have a lot of children, since he buys so much kids' stuff!" Dad smiled, continuing, "You don't know who he is, do you?" I said, "Yes, he is the ice and coal man."

Dad went on, "Yes he is, but there is more to Ezra. He is the preacher at the small storefront church down on Poplar Street. The church has about twenty adult church members. He has no children. The children's gifts are presents for the poor children in his congregation. Ezra hasn't much education, but I know that his congregation learns God's love from him. He knows the Bible and lives it, even when he sells ice and coal. Ezra is a real Christian."

When I think of the ministry of service as a focal point of the new evangelization, I remember Ezra. Early in my life, he showed me the meaning of Christian service. I never attended his church, but if his congregation followed his example, they could be likened to early Christian gatherings, where members came together, told the old, old story, broke bread, and went out and lived the message they heard.

The new evangelization proclaims a *ministry of service*. Jesus came to serve, and parishes continue his ministry. Christian service may include providing a loving, Christian atmosphere at home, offering a listening ear for a troubled colleague, or giving a loving response at work. Church-related groups — like the St. Vincent de Paul Society, the Legion of Mary, and the Daughters of Charity — do great work. So do high school students helping in a nursing home or a grandparent who advises a grandchild.

Living the message of Christian service means responding to needy people through acts of service, because they are children of God. *Sharing Catholic Social Teaching: Challenges and Directions* (CST) says, "Catholic social teaching is based on and inseparable from our understanding of human life and human dignity" (p. 1).

In old Ezra, I witnessed a man of human dignity, made in the image of God. Ezra saw this same dignity in every child, youth, and adult he met on the streets and touched through his church sermons. He reflected the words of *Sharing Catholic Social Teaching*: "[T]his commitment to social justice is at the heart of who we are and what we believe . . ." (p. 2). For this reason, we have no choice but to share and live it. We proclaim the Gospel's social mission because we believe every person is both sacred and social (CST, p. 4).

The call to evangelize is the special responsibility of pastoral ministers. Responding to it means following the Lord by hearing, proclaiming, celebrating, and responding to God's Word. Such action is at the heart of our identity as baptized Christians.

4. The New Evangelization and the Ministries of Word, Worship, and Service: Pastoral Reflections and Action Steps

This chapter reminds pastoral leaders of the significance of the Word of God, of celebrating it, and of serving others. We need to hear Jesus' words again and again. The following reflections and action steps invite pastoral ministers to remember their responsibilities and the opportunities they have to deepen their own "Amen" of faith and share it with others.

Pastoral Reflections

a. What childhood memories remind you of people who nourished your faith? Recall special times when your mother or father taught you to pray, read holy stories to you, or took you to church on Christmas or Easter? What do such memories say to you as a pastoral minister, as you think about your children or the children in the parish?

b. At what times do you feel too busy to pray and appreciate the working of God in your pastoral and personal lives? How can you encourage parishioners to be more faithful to Mass attendance and the celebration of the other sacraments?

c. What role does the *Rite of Christian Initiation of Adults* play in the new evangelization?

d. Have you ever been too preoccupied with your parish ministry, while you neglected your children, spouse, parents, or friends? Regardless of your answer, reflect on setting priorities in your life.

Action Steps

a. In what ways does your parish prepare parents to contribute to catechizing their children? What one important, easy-to-accomplish step could the parish take to improve this parental training?

b. What is the status of systematic catechesis in your parish? What steps might be taken to improve the parish's catechetical process?

c. What could your parish do to bring more people to faith in the real presence of Christ in the Eucharist?

d. What connection does your parish make between service and evangelization? What one important, easy-to-accomplish step could be taken to strengthen the connection?

Chapter Seven

The New Evangelization, Family, and Workplace

This chapter offers ways for parish leaders to help families grow in faith and for the parishioners to evangelize. In so doing, they become open books that unlock Christ's Good News for others. The chapter is divided into four sections. Section one discusses the Christian family as rooting the new evangelization. Section two looks at the new evangelization and the world where we live and work, and the third section considers challenges to the new evangelization in the family and broader society. Section four contains pastoral reflections and action steps.

The new evangelization challenges pastoral leaders to find creative ways to motivate parishioners to evangelize. This may require coordinated efforts in refocusing a parish's mission statement or priorities. It also means being more sensitive to the call to evangelize in every parish ministry. A pastor may need to be more attuned to show how his weekly homily connects with the needs of parishioners, or a deacon may renew his commitment to the parish's service to the poor and disenfranchised.

The new evangelization is intimately associated with ministry in the family and in the world. It cannot be emphasized enough that future Catholic vibrancy depends on how well parishes motivate parents to accept their responsibility to share Jesus' Good News in their families.

We begin with a story of my grandma.

When I was a small boy, Grandma put stale bread in the backyard for the birds, especially during snowstorms and gave away many of her possessions to those who needed them. Her love and gratitude for what she was blessed with filled me with a reverence for nature, animals, and people.

When thinking of her actions, I wonder if her early years — when, as a small child, she and her family had to leave Holland and take a boat to the United States — made her so compassionate and appreciative. She told me that on their voyage, they were housed at the bottom of the ship, with the baggage and other transported items, and how during a terrible storm, they had to throw most of their belongings overboard, lest the ship sink. Grandma also described her difficult early years in this country, when her mother, and then she, had to work as an upstairs maid for wealthy people. It seems as if what Grandma experienced led her to really appreciate nature and people, especially the least of God's creatures. As a small child, I loved my grandma and learned a great deal from her, even though she didn't have much schooling. In her simple ways — and through her compassion, gratitude, and love — she evangelized me.

My parents continued Grandma's good example. They provided a loving Catholic home, and as I grew, Dad and Mom read me Bible stories and taught me about Jesus. This reinforced Grandma's example from a redemption perspective. These experiences gave me a deep understanding of the kingdom of God, long before I discovered its meaning in the Bible.

Evangelization begins in Christian families. From the first seeds of faith, planted in family life, God's grace begins an unfolding process that lasts a lifetime. From a mother's smile to a father's sacrifice, God's spirit permeates a family, centered on love and faithfulness.

In this materialistic world, it is to our advantage to reflect on where and how God discloses life's meaning. It doesn't come through YouTube videos or new automobiles, but it is manifested in the love that family members show to one another.

The parish builds on the foundation set by the family. It provides resources for communal and personal catechesis, liturgical action, and support. Through the witness of pastoral leaders, a parish gives parishioners the courage to evangelize.

Catholic evangelization focuses on Jesus and finds expression in a parish. To be effective, a strong link must be established between the family, the world, and the parish as partners in evangelization.

Evangelization happens in everyday life. It is radically incarnational, meaning that God communicates through human exchange. The family and work in the world can be significant expressions of God's presence in society. They are vital focal points of the new evangelization.

1. The Christian Family: Rooting the New Evangelization

Because God is first disclosed in family life, evangelization begins here. As *On the Vocation and the Mission of the Lay Faithful in the Church and in the World* says, "The *Christian family*, as the 'domestic Church,' also makes up a natural and fundamental school for formation in the faith" (n. 62, emphasis in original).

Church documents use the term "family" to refer to "an intimate community of persons bound together by blood, marriage, or adoption, for the whole of life" (*A Family Perspective in Church and Society: A Manual for All Pastoral Leaders*, p. 17). This description includes nuclear, extended, single-parent, adoptive, and blended families. Single persons are included as part of a family.

My family experience taught me how birth, growth, joy, suffering, success, failure, life, and death root our relationship with God. In reflecting on my experiences, I recall the words of Ecclesiastes: "There is a season for everything. . . . A time for tears, a time for laughter; a time for mourning, a time for dancing" (3:1, 4; JB). While meditating on these words, I remember my father's last illness.

My father lay for months in a hospital bed. One cold January afternoon, Mom, my sisters Mary Ann and Joan, and I visited him. He smiled and asked for a wheelchair. Mom pushed him to the window. Mary Ann and I witnessed an epiphany of love as Dad and Mom held hands as the sun illuminated them. His wrinkles and strain were transformed by the intense peace they conveyed. They spoke softly. Mary Ann said, "Bob, seeing them together like this is worth all the long months of pain we have undergone." This moment disclosed how deep joy often comes after struggle and sacrifice.

As Dad and Mom sat there, it made no difference that his hair was not combed or that she wore an older dress. They were deeply present to one another; nothing else mattered. I saw how the most beautiful experiences happen in the simplest ways, and how God discloses divine beauty when simple people radiate unaffected love. When this happens, God gives freedom, couched in liberation from sin, pleasure, and worldly interests. This freedom invites healing and enables us to discover beautiful moments. Our common story allowed us to discover these moments. Indeed, there is a season for everything. That day with Mom and Dad was our time for beautiful moments.

People have different experiences of God's presence in families. This happens in nuclear families, blended families, or single-parent families. Family configurations often differ from my tightly knit, nuclear family. But whatever the family, most people experience God through familial love. I witnessed this love in Ed's story.

Ed, a mentally challenged man, began attending Mass in a parish where I ministered. I learned from a parishioner that he was baptized Catholic and wanted to receive Communion with the parish community, which welcomed him. Ed had no formal religious training, but to my surprise he knew the basics of the Catholic faith. I soon realized the depth of his understanding. After I asked him where he had learned about the Catholic faith and developed his positive outlook on life, Ed simply said, "From my grandmother. I have lived with her for thirty-three years. She taught me what I know."

Ed was deeply in love with God, and it would have been wrong to keep him from Communion any longer. The next Sunday he joyfully received his Lord, a practice that he continues to this day.

Christian families communicate aspects of God's presence by sharing the Christian faith within family life. The family is not an object "out there" to be evangelized by the Church. This attitude implies that the Church needs to teach families how to be families. It disregards the way God is present in a family relationship. It is far more accurate to say that families can teach the Church how to be Church. Family and Church are partners in evangelization.

Church documents, like the one quoted above, sometimes describe the *family* as the *domestic church* or the church of the home. *On the Vocation and the Mission of the Lay Faithful in the Church and in the World* says, "The daily life itself of a truly Christian family makes up the first 'experience of Church,' intended to find confirmation and development in an active and responsible process of the children's introduction into the wider ecclesial community and civil society" (n. 62). The family teaches moral values, guides children, maintains religious traditions, celebrates, prays, and supports its members in ways the parish cannot.

Pastoral ministers celebrate family life through Scripture, Church teaching, liturgy, and prayer. Parish schools and church activities help families grow in faith and link individual families with one another. *A Family Perspective in Church and Society* underlines the interconnectedness of family members, saying, "The family is not a collection of individuals, but a living and developing system whose members are essentially interconnected" (p. 8).

Pastoral ministers serve families by listening to their needs and responding to their requests. Often, preplanned or packaged programs may appeal to parish staffs but may mean little to families. As the *General Directory for Catechesis* says, "the Christian community must give very special attention to parents. By means of personal contact, meetings, courses and also adult catechesis directed toward parents, the Christian community must help them assume their responsibility — which is particularly delicate today — of educating their children in the faith" (n. 227).

Family members, by supporting one another, bring balance into a sometimes unbalanced society. Shari's story of a parent's support makes this clear.

Shari, a sixth-grade girl, came home laughing after a basketball game. She told her mom that her team lost, 25 to 5. Her mom asked, "What happened? Why are you laughing?"

Shari replied, "I feel great! We showed Mr. Zine, our grumpy basketball coach, who is the boss. He is always yelling at us to work harder and harder. He told us before the game that he was video recording us and we better do well. If not, he was going to let us have it, when we watched the video of our mistakes.

"I thought, 'He's not going to get away with that.' So I said to my teammates, 'It's not fair. After all, it's just a game. Let's really mess around, act like clowns, and have fun.' So we did and lost 25 to 5. We had a great time as he yelled and screamed. He was so embarrassed that he threw away the tape. He never knew what happened!"

The kids, sick of an adult demanding that they play like professionals, acted like kids. I sense God in the midst of this humor, clowning around in the children's hearts, laughing with them at the crabby, angry coach.

Shari's mom supported her, saying children's sports are supposed to be fun. She called the coach to let him know what she thought, suggesting that he look at his coaching methods. Imagine what might have happened if Shari's mom had not supported her. Her affirmation of Shari's conduct evangelized her daughter and reflected the way God supports us. If evangelization doesn't happen in families, how can it happen elsewhere?

2. The World Where We Live and Work

The term "world" is used broadly to include activities beyond the family and parish. It includes work, social involvement, neighborhood activities, and cultural activities. Such varied activities offer many possibilities to witness to God's presence and to evangelize others. This happens when we urge a colleague to trust God in a difficult situation or to show compassion to a neighbor. The college student who says no to another's sexual advances or the business executive who refuses a corporate deal that treats minorities unjustly, for example, evangelize by their actions.

A pastoral ministry retreat discussed Christian ministry in the market place, pointing out the responsibility to act charitably, honestly, and justly. Ed, an engineer, said that after the retreat he realized his obligation to avoid procedures that structurally weakened the products he designed. He followed up this decision as his ministry. His actions were received well, and eventually they influenced corporate policy.

Jeff, another retreat participant, laughed when Ed finished his story. He said, "My story is about upholding moral values, like Ed's, but it has a different ending. I was reassigned as assistant director of a large insurance office. After being there three months, I realized that unethical practices in our company hurt our clients. I spoke out against them.

"My boss, first reluctant to change, finally agreed. Things went along well. Office spirit improved, and profits increased. At the end of the fiscal year, we sent the main office our new procedures in the annual report. Then, something unexpected happened. Our operational mode threatened headquarters. One day, three corporate officers showed up unannounced, called together our office managers, and fired us. Then, the corporation assigned a new staff to take our place. Today the office is back to the same unjust procedures that we eliminated."

Jeff said that a Christian bold enough to evangelize in the market-place by acting ethically may face tough decisions and be rejected. He said that parish support, lacking in his case, is very important. "Rarely," he continued, "do we hear a homily or find a parish function that helps us sort out difficult moral issues in business. We need more moral guidance from our parish."

The Sacred and Secular World

A dichotomy often exists between the sacred (religion) and the secular (work and societal activities). When religion is confined to church services and prayer, it becomes disconnected from the rest of life. When this happens, it is difficult to integrate faith and daily living. People such as Jeff, seeking this integration, welcome parish support. For them, God is very much involved in what happens in the marketplace. It is sometimes difficult, however, to witness to the Good News without support from other Christians.

To provide such support, a Catholic organization — Ministry in the Marketplace — offered a monthly program for downtown business people. The sessions, held at noon in a corporate boardroom, centered on "Growing in Relationship with Self, Others, and God." About sixty people attended regularly. At its conclusion, the participants gave it high evaluations and made recommendations for future sessions.

Following their suggestions, the steering committee selected the theme of "Growing in Relationship: Implications for Family Life and Work" for the next sessions. When the sessions began, less than half the original group attended. Curious because of the request for follow-up sessions, the committee sought out the original members not in attendance, asking why they dropped out. Some answered that the topic was on target. If they attended, however, they would have to ask themselves hard questions about their families and work styles, which they were not ready to face. They seemed unwilling to risk hearing God's Word in the concrete world of their lives. They failed to appreciate that really listening to God's Word may require sacrifice, especially when hearing it might mean changing their lifestyles.

Evangelizing ministry in the world, amidst the secular pressures around us, is an important element for pastoral ministers to address. In some places, it may be the weakest aspect of parish ministry. It is seldom addressed in homilies or parish activities. Parish leaders need to acknowledge their responsibility to respond to this need, as a vital aspect of the new evangelization.

Our economy is geared around money. Sex sells, youth sells, Christmas sells. The Christmas season is the biggest sales event of the year.

Referring to inculturation, the *General Directory for Catechesis* says that "the Church must appropriate all the positive values of culture and of cultures (cf. EN 20; CT 53) and reject those elements which impede development of the true potential of persons and peoples" (n. 21). This is an important task for the Catholic evangelizer.

The new evangelization challenges us to look more deeply at the purpose of money and work. They are means to an end, not ends in themselves. They serve as instruments of God's kingdom, intended to help build the earth.

Ancient peoples knew that human labor was necessary to survive. They believed that life was sacred. For them, the primary emphasis was on family and tribe. Material possessions served the family, tribe, and God. In this way, early people balanced the ultimate and functional life dimensions.

Contemporary people often minimize human relationships and canonize things. A materialistic philosophy offers a bleak hope, for ultimate responses alone can adequately satisfy ultimate needs, manifested in the reciprocal love between spouses, parents, and children. When children receive functional responses to ultimate needs, exemplified by those who get a new toy instead of parental time and affection, the result may lead to alienation. If people do not receive ultimate responses to satisfy their ultimate needs, they will continue to hunger for something deeper.

Positive Elements

The contemporary world reflects many voices that cry out for justice and charity. They come from rich and poor, young and old. The Catholic evangelizer recognizes these cries, joins them, and links up with those who help the poor, volunteer at soup kitchens, and sacrifice personal comfort for families and neighbors. We find such people in supermarkets, classrooms, business offices, and shopping malls. They evangelize those about them.

From a different perspective, Jim, a math major in college, was inclined to switch his major. Many of his friends did volunteer work in the inner city, but he didn't have time to work with them. Because he felt he should do more for the poor, he thought about getting into social work. He hesitated, however, because he was getting all A's, and he really loved math.

I discussed Jim's concern with him. I said, "Only you can decide what to do. In your prayers, remember that God blessed you with mathematical talents and may be calling you to be the best mathematician you can be as your life's work. Consider all the people you could help if you use these talents to advance humankind by your contributions!"

Jim stayed in math and earned a Ph.D. degree. Now he is a professor at a large state-run university, is on numerous national and international commissions, and applies his Christian values to his work.

In his own way, Jim evangelizes, influencing decisions at a corporate level. This would not have been possible if he had not developed his mathematical gifts. His story invites us to use our God-given gifts to serve others. The Lord challenges us to clarify our calling, encouraging us to break down the barriers between faith and everyday life.

God invites pastoral ministers to make parishioners more aware of their calling to build the world in light of the kingdom. The shrinking of our world into a *global village* is a positive climate for the new evangelization. The technology explosion, rapid communication, television, computers, and the Internet have brought nations and races closer together and made us aware of human concerns around the world. These promise fresh opportunities for the new evangelization.

In coming together, our civilization can become more God-like. Reflecting on the world from the vantage point of faith, the *General Directory for Catechesis* says, "The Christian knows that every human event — indeed all reality — is marked by the creative activity of God which communicates goodness to all beings; the power of sin which limits and numbs man; and the dynamism which bursts forth from the Resurrection of Christ, the seed renewing believers is the hope of a definitive 'fulfillment' (GS 2). A world view not incorporating these three elements cannot be authentically Christian" (n. 16). These words challenge Catholic evangelizers in the world of tomorrow.

3. Today's Challenges to the New Evangelization in the Family and Broader Society

Society's nihilism, relativism, and materialism permeate life. Through interaction with friends, families, and work associates, we assimilate these "isms" almost by osmosis. Their tentacles infiltrate churches and schools. A good illustration of the latter happened in a Catholic parish.

The parish finance council report indicated that the parish's operating budget was $75,000 short for the coming year. After crunching the numbers, the council reduced the deficit by $10,000. This was not enough. Then, they took a bold step and recommended that the pastor fire all the support staff, including the secretary, the liturgist, and the catechetical leader, to balance the budget.

The pastor said, "I can't run the parish without them" and refused to let them go. At this, the matter got messy. The pastor, knowledgeable in financial matters, redid the budget, fired no one, and made the payroll the next year.

The sad thing about this whole affair is that the new evangelization was far from the thoughts of the finance council. Society's materialism and a "bottom line" mentality so affected them that they never saw real parish priorities.

With this said, let us consider challenges to evangelization in families and the workplace.

Challenges to Families

Parish leaders must take seriously the focus of the new evangelization when dealing with family life. Popes John Paul II and Benedict XVI reiterated this many times. Without a family focus, parish evangelization lacks a firm foundation. A question every parish must address is, "What can we do to strengthen family life and minister to family members in time of need?"

It's often difficult for family members to be together in the home at a given time of the day. Some work, others engage in sporting activities, still others pursue other events outside the home. This describes many "normal" families today. The new evangelization invites parents and family members, especially younger ones, to consider their priorities and the importance of spending time together at home.

Parish leaders must be particularly attentive to what challenges families. They cannot minister effectively when they act as if all parishioners are from integral, well-balanced families. Every Sunday, it is estimated that 50 percent or more of Mass attendees are from divorced families or know family members who are divorced. Some unmarried people attending Catholic churches live together with someone else. Often, they come to Mass and receive Communion, apparently thinking nothing of it. Still others engage in sexual activities outside of marriage or are actively involved in observing pornography. Such behavior strikes at the heart of a parish's moral life.

Pastoral ministers cannot take a heavy-handed approach in such matters, but neither can they avoid them as though they didn't exist. With great pastoral sensitivity, they need to address such issues. No parishioner is perfect and all of us are sinners, but there's a difference between acknowledging one's sins (and being forgiven) and acting as if sin does not exist.

When irregular situations are not addressed, the tone of the parish is affected. Scandalous actions on the part of parishioners provide a terrible example to other parishioners, especially the young. If parish leaders never address them, parishioners might conclude, "If nothing is said, they must not be so bad."

Family Faith

From marriage to baptismal preparation, parishes need to engage couples in serious discussions about the importance of faith in family life. Telling them about it is not enough. Pastoral leaders must do more to challenge spouses to see that their commitment to the faith affects how parents prepare their children to live their faith. Married couples need help to assist them in this effort.

Parish leaders can arrange for regular follow-ups after baptisms and marriages, inviting parents and family members to special events that support and encourage them. Attendance at such endeavors often is enhanced by personal invitations from family members or friends. When a friend invites a friend, or a neighbor invites a neighbor, or a family member invites another family member, there is more possibility that the person will come.

When parish leaders engage parishioners in Church activities and ministries, there is a better chance that such events will be well attended. Successful evangelical churches attract and maintain their members partially because of the active involvement of church members in the congregation's activities, especially when these assist the poor. They also attribute a member's staying power to his or her participation in small support groups that strengthen members to face everyday challenges.

Evangelizing at Work

Many students in a graduate "Theology of Ministry" course worked in various businesses. They developed creative projects in ministry centering on evangelizing others through giving example in the workplace.

Their commitment to Christ, witnessed by their working justly and acting kindly, impacted the attitudes of other workers. From them, we can learn that a great resource for pastoral leaders in addressing parishioners' needs in the workplace can be found by marshaling the wisdom of the working men and women sitting in church every Sunday. Much can be accomplished by directing the energy present in every parish congregation toward witnessing to Jesus' Good News in words and actions.

Pastoral leaders have a wealth of wisdom and information at their disposal. Many parishioners respond, if they are asked and motivated to act on Jesus' part. To do so, they need the parish's support to help them in their Christian service.

Great challenges exist for parish leaders to effectively evangelize families and the wider society. The new evangelization invites them to seriously consider these challenges.

4. The New Evangelization, Family, and Workplace: Pastoral Reflections and Action Steps

To appreciate the role of the family and the world in the new evangelization, the following pastoral reflections and actions steps are suggested.

Pastoral Reflections

a. In what ways does the experience of family life contribute to the new evangelization? What can families teach the Church about evangelization?

b. What do you think parishes can do to challenge parents to celebrate their faith openly in their families?

c. What might a parish do to help parishioners bridge the dichotomy between the sacred and the secular?

d. What are some of the challenges to evangelization in the family? In the workplace?

Action Steps

a. What does your parish do to help families evangelize their members? What one important, easy-to-implement step could the parish take to improve this effort?

b. What does your parish do to encourage and help parishioners bear witness to Christ and the Church in their environments? What could the parish do to strengthen this effort?

c. What does your parish do to prepare couples for marriage and family life? What could be done to strengthen this ministry and assure its contribution to the new evangelization?

d. What does your parish do to help young adults (ages eighteen to thirty-nine) find their vocation and to support them in dealing with the secular environments where they live, study, and work? Consider what the parish might do to improve its care for young adults.

Chapter Eight

The New Evangelization and Christian Spirituality

This chapter relates spirituality and the new evangelization to contemporary culture in four sections. Section one looks at spirituality and culture, and section two reflects on the new evangelization and spirituality. The third section looks at growth in Christian spirituality, and section four offers suggestions for pastoral reflections and action steps.

The new evangelization invites pastoral leaders to pattern their lives on Jesus. Living in his spirit is the heart of Christian spirituality. Parishioners see reflections of Jesus through the testimony of pastoral leaders and this motivates them to look further into the Good News. Their personal witness is a powerful reflection on the meaning of faith. It helps those with a secular bent to see life in a new way and turn from the world to God.

We begin with the story of the shingle cracker.

When walking around a folk festival, I saw booths of arts and crafts extending for two city blocks. In one booth, I spotted a beautiful painting of a thin old man with a wrinkled face and sun-dried hands, dressed in work clothes and holding a wooden mallet poised and ready to crack a shingle from a block of oak. Something about the picture of the old man struck me.

As I gazed at the picture, the booth keeper said: "It's really something, isn't it? The price is also something — two thousand dollars. The real shingle cracker lives near here. In fact, you can watch him crack shingles in a booth just over the hill to the right of my booth."

Interested in meeting the shingle cracker, I found him speaking to a small boy and his father. On one side of his booth were several hundred cracked shingles; behind them stood large oak tree trunks, cut into pieces the length of a wooden roof shingle. At the other end of the booth, the shingle cracker showed the boy how to crack a shingle. He put the wedge on the oak trunk, struck it with the mallet, and the shingle split off from the trunk.

The old man impressed me more than the picture. His worn hands showed two missing knuckles, possibly from a past accident with the mallet and wedge.

After the boy and his father left, I spoke with him. He said, "Did you see my picture?" When I said yes, he continued: "Yesterday, after they put it up, I went over and stood in back of the booth. Many people entered and admired it. When I heard their kind words, I tapped one fellow on the shoulder and said, 'The copy is great, but turn around and look at the original. It's better.' It was nice to see their smiles as they looked at me."

Then, his face grew sad, as he answered my question of how much the artist paid him to pose for the picture. He said, "I posed for over three hours and got fifty dollars." Then, he added, "There's something wrong with this — I got fifty dollars, and the artist will get two thousand dollars for putting lines on a canvas."

When I left him, I continued to think about how much the artist charged for the painting, which wouldn't have been possible without the original to portray. It struck me how often we put much more value on the copy than the original. Then, my thoughts turned to faith.

Humans, made in God's image, are beautiful copies of a divine image. Our beauty, however, fades when we fail to appreciate the original. It's never enough to stop with the copy, no matter how splendid. To appreciate another person, we must return to God, and see the divine image shining in everyone. For Christians, the original is Jesus. By living his example, we discover life's meaning.

The new evangelization demands that we look to Jesus, the original, and pattern our lives after him. In doing so, we become like the original. As St. Paul says, "I live now not with my own life but with the life of Christ who lives in me" (Galatians 2:20; JB). This is the heart of life and the basis of Christian spirituality.

1. Spirituality and Culture

God seeks us from our birth. Our response at various life stages affects our spirituality, for spirituality is the way that the Holy Spirit enters, permeates, and changes our lives.

The new evangelization, closely related to spirituality, connects with our experience of the beauty of life and parental love. God's created world touches our innermost being, as families, friends, and parishes nourish God's presence. From them, we receive care, support, and affirmation. We can love because loving, caring people reached out to us.

Culture has a powerful influence on spiritual formation. I grew up in a Catholic family and neighborhood, attended Catholic schools, and took an active part in parish functions. During these years, my spirituality deepened, because of my family's faith and our parish's support. Church rituals and personal prayer were hallmarks of Catholic spirituality at this time.

Efforts to facilitate spiritual growth in a family, school, or parish must be sensitive to an individual's spiritual tendencies. Where such sensitivity is absent, negative results usually follow. For example, Maria, a Hispanic woman, entered a convent but lasted only one year. She found it difficult to integrate her spiritual traditions with the community's white, middle-class values. In the past, African-American men entering seminaries often had a similar reaction.

Regardless of cultural pressures, a force greater than ourselves carries us along. Absolute trust in this greater force (God) directing human life is the moving force for spiritual growth. Who can say why some receive this or that gift, this or that opportunity? Why do others have to suffer so much? We cannot adequately answer these questions, but we know from our Christian faith that God supports and loves every person. When faced with difficulties, God will never abandon us.

In whatever circumstance we find ourselves, belief in God's presence is a powerful motivating force that can keep us going. When we remain confident that God is with us, God's divine presence becomes a strong rudder guiding us into the future. At such times, faith roots our Christian spirituality. By saying yes to the Holy Spirit within us, we carry out God's divine will for us.

Christian spirituality involves our ongoing response to the Spirit, as he invites us to enter more deeply into the life of the Trinity and to reach out to share the Good News. It is rooted in the Paschal Mystery and filtered through the Church.

2. The New Evangelization and Spirituality

Pre-Vatican II spirituality stressed following God's will by obeying Church beliefs and carrying out her practices. At the Second Vatican Council, spirituality shifted focus, as the Council Fathers stressed giving top priority to living in God's kingdom. These two types of spirituality — one based on obedience, the other rooted in God's Spirit moving us to do good — are not mutually exclusive. Their ultimate goal is union with God, but their approaches differ.

Linking spirituality with the new evangelization means that spirituality:

- Focuses on the kingdom.
- Needs the Christian community to support the kingdom focus.
- Acknowledges God's presence in family, marketplace, and society.
- Accepts God's creative activity in the world.
- Responds to Jesus' call to challenge unjust social and Church structures.
- Bases its orientation on Baptism and the common priesthood of all Christians.
- Recognizes the need for sacred time to pray and reflect.
- Develops a close bond with the Church's liturgical and sacramental life.
- Connects God's presence in life with God's biblical Word.
- Places high regard on spiritual reading and Church teaching as solid grounding for spirituality.

These dimensions of Christian spirituality invite pastoral ministers to examine how the parish helps its members grow in faith. The heart of this quest involves listening and responding to God.

The Role of Story

Often, we find that our stories tell us something about the way we do things. This came home to me not long after my ordination. Mom attended a Mass where I was the celebrant. Afterward, in discussing my apparently uninspiring homily, she said, "Bob, tell stories." Her words were like the Lord himself telling me to link the Scriptures with life.

I followed her advice. When I began telling stories, my preaching changed. "Why does everyone listen," I wondered, "when a story is told? Why do they get distracted with more technical explanations?" Soon, I realized that a story appeals to the whole person — emotions, spirit, and mind — while explanations or examples appeal primarily to the mind. In the depths of our story, we can find God.

Native Americans remind us of the importance of stories. For them, *the story* frames life. Creation stories, hero myths, and other tribal stories set the parameters for their existence. These stories explain why things are as they are and make fuller sense than rational analysis alone.

Spirituality is enhanced by the wisdom of others who listen to our stories. This happens in spiritual companioning, shared faith experiences, and retreats. These gatherings invite us to find God in our lives. Parish efforts to enhance parishioners' spirituality are inadequate if they fail to help people sort out the Spirit's role in their work, family, and social life.

Spirituality, centered on our stories, provides a focal point for the new evangelization, enabling us to develop a value system from within, rather than having one imposed from without.

Spiritual Maturity

Spirituality based on our story brings us to spiritual maturity. Becoming spiritually mature is lifelong. Some fourteen-year-olds are spiritually mature for their age, while some forty-year-olds are spiritually immature. Respecting our uniqueness means acknowledging the personal and social factors operative in our spiritual growth.

To become spiritually mature, we must reach out to life. Small babies move their hands and arms. Toddlers explore their surroundings. Adolescents begin a search to find themselves. Adults move into a wide variety of experiences that connect them with their inner selves and with others. This reaching out is essential to probe life's mysteries and appreciate God's presence.

When I was a boy, my family supported, affirmed, and loved me. Dad and I played ball, our family went on vacations, and Mom helped me with homework. In grade and high school, this supportive environment continued. I developed self-confidence and a positive outlook amidst the ups and downs of growing toward maturity. During this growth stage, I began to learn who I was. Acceptance by family, school, and neighbors helped me sort this out in ways that a child and adolescent can. I put rejection by a few classmates in the broader context of a loving environment.

When I went to the seminary, my early nurturing environment changed. The seminary's rigor and competition contrasted sharply with my home. One day, I was ridiculed by a professor. Shredded by his words, my confidence was shattered. This event made me insecure when speaking publicly. For twelve years, I fell into a falsetto tone in public speeches. Finally, four years after ordination, after moving into a supportive environment, I returned to my natural speaking ways.

Success, affirmation, disappointment, and failure influence our self-image on a subconscious level. Self-reflection, or taking the time to ask questions about who we are and how events affect us, helps us grow toward spiritual maturity. The ever-present God — reflected by the positive actions of family members, friends, and counselors — moves us to new levels of spiritual awareness.

Through self-reflection, we come to clearer personal insights. This recognition is basic for a mature spiritual life.

3. Growth in Spirituality

Spirituality, based on the kingdom of God, takes various shapes, depending on the time, culture, environment, group, and individual.

We crave direction, certitude, and roots, which our faith offers us. Catholic beliefs and practices, rooted in Jesus' teaching on the kingdom of God, acknowledge personal freedom and invite us to live the Christian life.

Our growth to spiritual maturity is foundational to the new evangelization. This means:

- Knowing Jesus' teaching on the kingdom.
- Appreciating Catholic beliefs and practices.
- Making Jesus and the parish important aspects of our life.
- Acknowledging family and work as central places to share faith.
- Developing a spirituality that integrates personal life, family, work, society, and Church into a holistic perspective.
- Giving Christian witness.

- Inviting others, through deeds and words, to follow Jesus in the Catholic faith.
- Acknowledging God's presence in culture, other Christian denominations, the Jewish faith, and world religions.
- Making Christian values unifying factors in our personal and communal life.
- Recognizing the presence of the living Lord at the heart of our family and the basis for our union with God.

Christian spirituality invites us to share our faith in our family, to struggle for justice, and to participate in missionary activities. A spiritually mature person's life revolves around faith, which challenges the individual to focus on love, justice, mercy, and compassion.

Jesus was fully human and fully divine and is our model for spiritual maturity. Seeing it this way implies that:

- Christian spirituality situates our relationship with God and the world.
- Christian spirituality links us with Jesus through his teaching on the kingdom. A kingdom-based spirituality sees healing and forgiveness as center points linking broken humanity with God. Striving to become fully human means loving God, serving others, and working for justice.
- Christian spirituality is a lifelong quest. The prologue of John's Gospel describes the Word (Jesus) as existing from the beginning and revealing himself in time. For the Christian, this means that we are on a spiritual journey, accompanied by Jesus, seeking ultimate unity with God in heaven.
- Christian spirituality is alive with God's Spirit. It motivates us to action by stressing our vocation to share God's life with others. A spirituality based in faith brings energy into our active search for meaning.
- Christian spirituality treats people of other races and religions as God's children, acknowledges different methods of prayer, and allows for diversity. The spiritually mature person recognizes the whole world as the arena of God's presence.
- Christian spirituality is open to change and eager to investigate our faith. It overcomes fear with faith and guilt with love, and learns from various religious and secular sources.

- Christian spirituality recognizes all people as equal before God. This leads to dialogue, where others are respected, not controlled or manipulated. It also acknowledges that God's love is filtered through human love, which begins in God.
- Christian spirituality brings new insights, for it discerns our activities in light of God's revelation and Church teaching. A spiritually mature person recognizes the Holy Spirit as the ultimate source of our wisdom.
- Christian spirituality admits human limits and sees the humor in an all-powerful God becoming human and dying for sinful creatures. It also acknowledges God's playfulness, patience with weak human beings, and tolerance of failure, as well as God's justice, fairness, and truth. This humorous and playful characteristic of spirituality reminds the spiritually mature person that we are human and that God is God.
- Christian spirituality finds its apex in the communal celebration of Jesus' Paschal Mystery in the Eucharist and the other sacraments.

The new evangelization finds its deepest meaning in our spiritual quest, where God's presence reaches fulfillment on earth. Our faith life bears fruit to the degree that we respond to the spiritual yearnings of our heart. Here, God is present and fully alive.

When we experience God's love in the love we have for one another and share this love in word and deed, Christian spirituality energizes the new evangelization. The Christian message is taught, celebrated, and lived when Jesus' way of love becomes our way of love, for human love is the deepest manifestation of his Good News.

4. The New Evangelization and Christian Spirituality: Pastoral Reflections and Action Steps

Pastoral Reflections

a. How do cultural and family circumstances affect a person's spirituality? In what ways can a pastoral leader help people overcome cultural obstacles to their spiritual growth?

b. What role does "story" play in a person's growth to spiritual maturity?

c. What does it mean to say that our growth to spiritual maturity is foundational for the new evangelization?

d. How does your personal spirituality influence the way you do evangelization? How does it influence the way you help others evangelize?

Action Steps

a. Schedule a morning or evening of reflection for the staff and ask each pastoral leader to share his or her personal story of faith and spiritual growth. Open with Scripture and song, and close with Benediction.

b. Ask the pastoral staff to spend a month reading and reflecting each day on a portion of the Gospel of Mark. At the end of the month, set aside time at a meeting for each pastoral leader to share how reflecting on Mark touched her or his life.

c. Invite parishioners to a one-hour-long teaching event that focuses on the importance of prayer and personal spiritual growth as the foundations for effective evangelization.

d. Consider holding quarterly parish-wide evenings of prayer for inactive Catholics. The service could include worship songs, Scripture readings, teaching, testimony, prayer for relatives and friends, and Benediction.

Chapter Nine

The New Evangelization and Conversion

This chapter considers conversion and the new evangelization in five sections. The first section looks at faith and conversion, and the second explores kinds of conversion. Section three looks at facilitating conversion, and section four considers methods of conversion. Section Five presents pastoral reflections and action ideas.

The term "conversion" is sometimes associated with joining a church. More often, it means growing more deeply in our relationship with the Lord, and how we allow the Spirit of the risen Lord to dwell within and change us. In this sense, conversion is a lifelong process.

Like spirituality, conversion is ongoing, as we deepen and refocus our attitudes, energies, life patterns, and loyalties in light of Jesus and Church teachings. Conversion is part of our lifelong journey to God.

1. Faith and Conversion

The *General Directory for Catechesis* relates faith and conversion. It says, "Faith involves a change of life, a *'metanoia'* (cf. EN 10; AG 13b; CCC 1430-1431) that is a profound transformation of mind and heart; it causes the believer to live that conversion (EN 23)" (n. 55). The document continues, "By meeting Jesus Christ and by adhering to him the human being sees all of his deepest aspirations completely fulfilled" (n. 55).

Evangelization is associated with the invitation from God to change, and conversion involves the response in faith.

Conversion, like evangelization, can be implicit or explicit. *Implicit conversion* means developing positive attitudes toward life or changing one's outlook as a result of one's experiences with life itself without explicit references to God. The following stories reflect implicit conversion.

When I was a small boy, two events affected my outlook toward life. The first happened when I was in the first grade. I became sick, and the doctor said I had to stay home from school all year. He said I would have to take the first grade over. When Mom heard this, she went to my teacher, got my books, and began teaching me. Every day, she spent hour after hour teaching me to spell, read, write, and add. Her goodness, patience, and love gave me confidence. Each afternoon, Mom walked to school, talked to the teacher to get the lessons for the next day. When I returned to school at the end of the year, I was way ahead of the rest of the class and moved to the second grade with them.

The second event happened three years later. During World War II, a group of neighbors planted Victory gardens in the empty lot behind our home. A successful businessman, who lived up the street and grew up on a farm, befriended me. He taught me how to prepare the soil for planting, plant various crops, prune tomatoes, grow pole beans, and hoe radishes.

Sam, an old man, had a patch of tomato plants in his garden where the soil was rocky. Every day, he watered his plants, tried to hoe them, and waited for tomatoes. But only small green ones appeared on the vines, soon to wither from lack of nourishment. The old man kept watching for red tomatoes, but they never came. His eyesight was not good, and sometimes I tried to help him find red tomatoes on his plants.

One day my businessman friend said, "Bob, we are going to assist nature and make old Sam happy. Only a miracle will put ripe tomatoes on his plants. So we'll help make this miracle happen."

He took some nice red tomatoes from his garden and left about two inches of green stem on each tomato. Then we went to old Sam's patch and tied the ripe tomatoes on Sam's plants with very thin green thread. When Sam discovered the ripe tomatoes, he called me over and said, "I'm satisfied now, because I have ripe tomatoes."

What my businessman friend did for old Sam stuck with me and manifested a facet of human kindness. In retrospect, I know that God was present in our act of kindness. As I grew, experiences like these influenced me. Positive reactions to such events influenced my implicit conversion. Such implicit conversion events are doors that afford further opportunities for explicit conversion for those who are desirous of growing in faith, for the unchurched, or for those who have left the Church for various reasons.

Explicit conversion directly relates to God the Father, Jesus, or the Holy Spirit in some way. It identifies God's presence on our life journey and how we need to turn to him in prayer. This awareness comes gradually. During the months I stayed home from school in the first grade, Mom taught me about God's love, helped me trust him, and prayed with me. Slowly the implicit conversion I learned from her goodness became more explicit, as I sensed God's presence healing me while she taught me about Jesus.

In the same way, years after the Victory garden experience of tying tomatoes on Sam's stalks, I learned that being a Christian means helping people, as my friend and I had helped Sam. The gardening experience taught me to see God's all-encompassing providence everywhere. As my early experience of implicit conversion became explicit, I connected these childhood events with God and his kingdom.

2. Kinds of Conversion

People come to conversion in different ways. *Gradual conversion* happens in life's give and take from childhood to old age. Most people come to God in this way and can point to no single event as a definitive moment of conversion. Gradual conversion usually happens in imperceptible ways, as the Lord gently calls us to discipleship.

A paradigm of such conversion is found in the story of Samuel, where God calls him four times. Finally, Samuel recognizes the call, after he has spoken to Eli, the prophet, several times. Then, as Eli instructed him, the next time God calls him, Samuel replies, "Speak, for your servant is listening" (1 Samuel 3:10; see Samuel 3:1-10, 19; NRSV). In a similar way, the Lord called Peter, Andrew, and most of his apostles and disciples (John 1:35-51). It took them a long time to realize the full implications of their calling. The same is true in our journey to God. Often, it takes quite a while for us to recognize God's call. Usually we need the help of another, as Samuel did, to recognize it.

Radical conversion refers to conversion experiences of a definite kind, when a person can point to a specific experience that dramatically altered his or her life. Jesus called Paul in this way (Acts 9:1-18). On the road near Damascus, a light surrounded him, and the Lord spoke to him. Falling to the ground, Saul experienced a sudden, radical encounter with Jesus that changed him. With that, Paul became a new person.

Often, radical and gradual conversions occur together. The gradual process of conversion may be affected by radical events that force a person to rapidly change focus. Even radical conversion can be ongoing, as we gradually integrate such traumatic experiences into life's overall framework.

Sometimes, a traumatic experience challenges one's attitude toward faith. Some people find the Lord through such an event. This happened to Jim. He had no active faith, though he was raised a Catholic. Then, his child developed a rare disease that immobilized her. This changed Jim's outlook, and he became a devout believer, who impressed others by the way he cared for his child. His child's sickness deeply changed him.

At other times, difficult experiences can lead to loss of faith. This happened in the case of a woman who never attended church again after her child's sudden death. Previously, this woman went to Mass regularly.

Many key moments in the conversion process converge around significant rites of passage. Positive ones may include a child's birth, beginning school, First Communion, graduation from elementary and secondary school, getting a driver's license, marriage, or a grandchild's birth. Negative experiences may include a family member's death, divorce, sickness, job loss, or old age.

A deeper understanding of life's mystery centered on faith and a greater commitment to love God and neighbor are goals of conversion. As we mature spiritually, it becomes clear to us that full happiness cannot be realized on earth. As St. Augustine said, *"Our hearts are restless, and they cannot rest until they rest in you, O God"* (*Confessions*, Book 1, Chapter 1). The journey to God has many ups and downs. These peaks and valleys jar us into deeper appreciation of life's ultimate purpose and trigger implicit and explicit conversion.

Continuing Christian conversion is a gradual process, growing in intensity as we allow the Holy Spirit to change us. It has one aim: "a complete and sincere adherence to Christ and his Gospel through faith. Conversion is a gift of God, a work of the Blessed Trinity" (*On the Permanent Validity of the Church's Missionary Mandate* [RM], n. 46).

Inspired by the Spirit, who "opens people's hearts," life experiences are constantly reintegrated into a person's personality as one deepens, shifts, or changes life's priorities (RM, n. 46).

Life events have varying degrees of significance, but God is present in all of them. Hence, Christian conversion means taking on the mind and heart of Jesus, as we grow to appreciate God's role in our life. The *General Directory for Catechesis* stresses continuing conversion when it says, "Faith is a gift destined to grow in the hearts of believers (CT 20a: 'It is in fact a matter of giving growth, at the level of knowledge and in life, to the seed of faith sown by the Holy Spirit with the initial proclamation'). Adhering to Jesus Christ, in fact, sets in motion a process of continuing conversion, which lasts for the whole of life (cf. RM 46b)" (n. 56).

Conversion sets the foundation for Christian discipleship. It involves deepening our realization of the meaning of Jesus' command to *Love God and one another.* As conversion intensifies, we see better our call to discipleship through the lens of this great commandment. As our attitudes and actions change, we grow to recognize the implications of living this commandment.

Conversion also helps us discover the special gifts that God gives us. In using these gifts as, say, a laborer, teacher, computer operator, nurse, businessperson, writer, contractor, student, or waiter, we come to recognize work as an opportunity to proclaim God's evangelizing Word.

Conversion invites us to see more deeply how God's call to discipleship applies to family life. In discerning the Lord's call, we pay particular attention to the family aspect of Christian discipleship.

Since the transcendent God does not operate the way we do, conversion has many faces and cannot be programmed. One experience that changed my spiritual focus happened in the simplest way.

After a retreat, I spent another day in silent recollection. My life was going well. There were pressures, concerns, and irritations, but I was happy and fulfilled. I went to bed late that night. Early the next morning, while waking up, a powerful experience overcame me. Immediately I arose and jotted an expression on a piece of torn paper to remember the experience. Had I not, the event would have been lost. I wrote: "This morning, I came to an awareness that I was being touched by a reality so deep that my whole inner self became suffused with meaning." As the *General Directory for Catechesis* says, "Faith and conversion arise from the '*heart*,' that is, they arise from the depth of the human person and involve all that he is" (n. 55, emphasis in original).

A goal of conversion is to connect us with the saving graces won by Jesus. The *General Directory for Catechesis* (n. 56b) speaks of this when it says,

> The option for faith must be a considered and mature one. Such searching, guided by the Holy Spirit and the proclamation of the *Kerygma*, prepares the way for conversion which is certainly "initial" (AG 13b), but brings with it adherence to Christ and the will to walk in his footsteps. This "fundamental option" is the basis for the whole Christian life of the Lord's disciple (cf. AG 13; EN 10; RM 46; VS 66; RCIA 10).

3. Facilitating Conversion

The new evangelization plays a vital role in how parish leaders address conversion, which can happen *individually* and relate to the personal faith journey of individuals, or *communally* as a whole community or group of Christians journey together toward their salvation. Our communal walk with God begins in families and is supported by Christian believers.

Parish efforts to facilitate conversion need to center on what meaning Jesus' teaching can have on people's lives, for our relationship with God roots our meaning. Although conversion involves a personal search, community is central to it. In community, God is disclosed and a person is supported.

In stressing *community* in adult faith formation, *Adult Catechesis in the Christian Community* (ACICC), published by the International Council for Catechesis, states, "One of the most valid criteria in the process of adult catechesis, but which is often overlooked, is the *involvement of the community* which welcomes and sustains adults" (n. 28, emphasis in original). These words challenge every parish to maintain a healthy balance between individual and communal conversion in its ministry.

Pastoral ministers can help facilitate conversion in catechetical ministry, RCIA, youth ministry, Bible sharing, and adult faith discussion groups. Recognizing diverse Catholic populations reinforces the need for flexible methods to facilitate it.

Helping others on their faith journey implies that parish ministers need to acknowledge God's presence in all aspects of the parish. A pastoral leader facilitates another's conversion by helping the individual recognize the presence of the living God and developing methods to assist people in their journey to God.

4. Conversion and Methods

A difference exists between conversion and methods to facilitate it. Made possible by divine grace, conversion happens between God and a person or a community. For a pastoral leader, conversion is the goal, and methods are means to attain this goal.

No one best method exists to enhance parishioners' conversion. Various methods can be used at different phases of the conversion process. As the *General Directory for Catechesis* says, "The Church, in transmitting the faith, does not have a particular method nor any single method" (n. 148). Effective methods take into account the person, the environment, and the facilitator's gifts. Patience, understanding, love, and trust are at the heart of every method.

Family faith grows in ordinary and special circumstances. Mutual forgiveness and love cement family ties and invite ongoing conversion. Formal methods, like teaching children the Our Father or having an Advent wreath, deepen the conversion happening through family relationships.

Methods are secondary to conversion itself. Saying the family Rosary after dinner may be a more useful method in some families than in others. Attendance at Sunday liturgy may be seen differently by various family members. If a teenager refuses to attend Sunday Mass, a parent, after a serious discussion with the teen, might conclude that the young person is not lazy but is struggling with a faith problem. In such cases, a parent might help a son or daughter grow in faith by discussing Scripture and applying its message to the teenager's life. Gradually, this can lead to a better appreciation of the Mass and regular attendance. Sometimes, parents enforce rules without looking at the root problem.

What works with one person may not be useful for another. Hence, the RCIA and catechetical ministry need to employ flexible methods. When flexibility is lacking, we risk absolutizing a method. Then, the method can seem more important than conversion itself.

Since we use different methods to facilitate conversion, selecting a method depends on the people involved. In one instance, a method centering on prayer or Scripture may be the most effective one. In another, a didactic approach may be better. In speaking of adaptation, the *General Directory for Catechesis* states, "Adaptation is realized in accordance with the diverse circumstances in which the word of God is transmitted (cf. RM 33). . . . It shall be remembered that, in the plurality of situations, adaptation must always keep in mind the totality of the person and his essential unity . . ." (n. 170).

We come to God differently. Sometimes we need time alone to enhance our conversion. At other times, we may prefer limited group interaction or more intense dialogue. Such personal preferences influence how we relate to God and others. Because our attitudes affect the conversion process, methods and content materials need to connect with where people are.

In communal conversion, we distinguish natural groups (separated and divorced people or children who have lost a parent) from more random groups (a youth catechetical group or an adult enrichment program). A common concern links natural groups; random groups have no such binding force. Such differences are significant in selecting a method. One method may work best for a given group, leading people to deeper faith, better appreciation of community, and more profound links with God. Conversion is the bottom line in selecting any method, not the method itself.

Conversion centers on our search for God in a fractured world, where common brokenness is the starting point. Here, Jesus offers healing and leads us to life's core dimension, where God dwells. Today's complex world invites us to return to the Gospel message of love. Here, we recognize people's diversity and evangelize in light of it. We proclaim the Good News, as we remember how Jesus taught. He preached a message, often in story form, and challenged his hearers to consider its consequences. We evangelize, as we find new meaning in his Word-made–flesh.

5. The New Evangelization and Conversion: Pastoral Reflections and Action Steps

To help become more sensitive to conversion moments, we are invited to reflect and act, based on notions gleaned from this chapter.

Pastoral Reflections

a. Reflect on a moment of conversion in your family or among relatives or friends. What circumstances influenced the conversion? Was it gradual or radical? Did the person respond with continuing change and growth? What does this person's experience teach you about conversion and the new evangelization?

b. What is *implicit conversion*? How have you seen it work in the lives of people who are being evangelized?

c. What actions can pastoral leaders take to facilitate conversions among members of the parish?

d. What role does the parish community play in facilitating conversion?

Action Steps

a. Spend ten minutes at the beginning of each staff meeting discussing new evangelization in the parish, paying special attention to how well the community is facilitating conversion among its members.

b. Have the pastoral leaders of the RCIA share with the staff what they have learned about conversion in caring for candidates and catechumens in the process.

c. Use a retreat or another means to foster conversion within the parish. For example, consider using Christ Renews His Parish (www.mycrhp.org) or Discovering Christ (www.ChristLife.org).

d. Hold annual or semi-annual days or weekends of reflection for the pastoral staff. Include time for prayer for parishioners, personal sharing, Scripture, and silent reflection. Invite a speaker to teach about the elements of the new evangelization.

Chapter Ten

The New Evangelization — Catholic Style

To address the characteristics of the new evangelization, this chapter is divided into two main sections. The first section describes ten chief characteristics of the new evangelization and draws implications for Catholic parishes. The second main section offers suggestions for pastoral reflections and action steps.

The new evangelization differs from Protestant evangelism. The latter often focuses on sharing the Good News in such a way that it leads to Christ in a definitive moment, whereby a person is converted or saved. The new evangelization recognizes that the proclamation of the Good News is a lifelong enterprise and must be adapted to the times and circumstances. It is radically incarnational, based in the Trinity, community directed, ecclesially balanced, and integrates Church ministry with life. In addition, it is biblically and kingdom centered, dynamically holistic, optimistic, but realistic, Spirit led, process oriented, integral to peoples' lives, constant but consistent in orientation, socially conscious, and dependent on the Holy Spirit.

I. Characteristics of Catholic Evangelization

Even though changes at Vatican II eliminated many traditional customs, distinctive Catholic expressions remain in biblical interpretation, ecclesiology, hierarchical structure, ministry, sacraments, and morality. The following characteristics of Catholic evangelization, rooted in God's saving love, are of special significance.

1. Radically Incarnational

Catholic evangelization happens in the midst of everyday life. God communicates through sunsets, mountains, birds, plants and people. In particular, God comes through humans, created in the divine image. Blessed John Paul II says that humans are "called to a fullness of life which far exceeds the dimensions of his earthly existence, because it consists in sharing the very life of God" (*The Gospel of Life*, n. 2). The Christian community helps communicate Jesus' message by illuminating God's presence in life.

Family, world, and Church are primary disclosure points for God's presence and Christian evangelization. Jesus is present to us in Word and sacrament. Family, friends, society, work, science, neighbors, technology, and business are fruitful places to discover God's presence or share Jesus' message. A parish, diocese, or religious community gathers us to hear, celebrate, and respond to God's Word and to serve others.

2. Trinitarian and Community-Directed

Catholic evangelization is rooted in the Trinity and centered in community. It is not a "me and Jesus" experience. From our earliest years, we learn about God through people. We are called as *a people* to follow Jesus, who himself gathered a community of disciples.

Evangelization's first witness comes through community, usually the family. We seek a personal relationship with the Triune God in union with our brothers and sisters in faith.

Evangelization creates a welcoming spirit in Christian homes and parishes. We find Good News in our families and at church. Such news begins when we feel important and know others are glad we are present. Day-to-day exchanges between family members let us know that we are loved. Parishes have unique opportunities to express such love at Sunday liturgies, weddings, funerals, baptisms, and special gatherings. The way parish members conduct meetings, answer the phone or doorbell, and send out communications speaks to the parish's belief in Jesus' Good News.

Evangelization that stresses personal conversion and fails to take into account the community dimension of faith is incomplete. *Thy Kingdom Come* indicates the importance of community, saying, "Catholics believe they embrace the fullness of the incarnation when they embrace Jesus in the most intimate communion with his body, the Church" (p. 3).

3. Ecclesially United

Catholic evangelization recognizes the Holy Spirit's presence in the pope, the Church hierarchy, and the entire ecclesial community. This union enables Jesus' message to be proclaimed faithfully and completely. From the beginning of Christian times, apostles and bishops, given the mission of preserving Jesus' authentic teachings, directed the Church, as heresies threatened to split it apart. This mission continues today under the leadership of the pope and the Magisterium.

This is important for the new evangelization. The Church continues to have lay prophets and teachers, ministering in the body of believers, under the Magisterium's guidance. This dynamic within the Church ensures fidelity to God's Word and avoids one-sided interpretations that characterize the "me and Jesus" approach to individual conversion.

The Holy Spirit creates the bond of unity, joining the pope, bishops, clergy, religious, and laity. The heart of evangelizing efforts rests in the laity, working in conjunction with the entire Church. Through the Spirit-given gifts of members, the Church community builds up the Body of Christ and announces its vibrant presence to the world.

4. Biblically Comprehensive

While Catholic evangelization teaches that all Scripture is God's revealed Word, it does so in a comprehensive way, taking into account social and cultural factors that influenced a given text. A passage's meaning is best understood in light of its purpose, primary audience, and literary form. Because these are not always clear, we receive guidance from the hierarchy, Tradition, magisterial teaching, and scholarly research. We have the Church's authority to support our interpretation of biblical texts, as we study Scripture, pray with it, and deepen our faith.

While at its core God's Word never changes, Catholic evangelization applies it to various life circumstances. In so doing, Scripture illuminates our experiences and gives us insights into life's meaning.

5. Kingdom-Centered

Catholic evangelization centers on the kingdom of God, announced by Jesus. His kingdom focuses on bringing health and salvation to those whose lives are broken economically, physically, psychologically, and spiritually. Evangelization acknowledges the kingdom's presence in everyday life and inspires us to perform acts of Christian service. Jesus' proclamation of the kingdom begins in this life and ultimately leads to salvation, which is the enjoyment of eternal happiness with God in heaven.

To say that the primary goal of Catholic evangelization is to *make new Church members* is one-sided. This narrow approach can lead to proselytization. While inviting others into the Catholic community, we remember that God's kingdom is broader than the Catholic Church.

Reconciliation and ministry to broken people are signs of God's kingdom in our midst. Catholics reject evangelistic efforts that consider earthly success or wealth as righteous signs of God's special favor. Catholics, instead, place special emphasis on social justice.

6. Dynamically Holistic

Based in God's kingdom, Catholic evangelization motivates a community to proclaim the living Christ through the ministries of word, worship, and service. Church organizations, structures, and programs assist the parish's evangelization outreach. These do not operate effectively in isolation. Catechesis, liturgy, and social action overlap, even though these ministries are based respectively in the ministries of word, worship, and service.

Catholic evangelization is one process with different aspects. Proclaiming God's Word is integrally related to prayer. Eucharist actions flow from the Paschal Mystery and coalesce into a holistic vision of God's Word, celebrated in a vibrant faith life. The *General Directory for Catechesis* emphasizes the integral notion of evangelization, when it states, "Evangelization, too, which transmits Revelation to the world, is also brought about in words and deeds. It is at once testimony and proclamation, word and sacrament, teaching and task" (n. 39).

7. Optimistic But Realistic

Catholic evangelization, while acknowledging the reality of sin, rests on the premise that the world is basically good. God created a good world, and humans are fundamentally good. Moral evil, or sin, disrupts this harmony. The second creation story in Genesis (Genesis 2:5ff.) addresses the question of evil. It promises eventual salvation to the righteous. This came to humankind through the person of Jesus, the Son of God. Creation after the Fall remains good but wounded. In this condition of sin and salvation, the all-holy God guides a good world, and the risen Lord lives in the Christian community.

Catholics reject the belief that the fall of Adam and Eve rendered creation inherently corrupt. This attitude focuses on sin and minimizes human goodness. While not downplaying the power of sin, Catholic evangelization concentrates on God's grace, which offers freedom and hope. In all salvation history, God urges people to reject sin, repent, forgive, and begin anew.

8. Spirit-Led

Jesus sent the Holy Spirit to guide the Church, and in turn, the Christian parish. In John, we read, "The Advocate, the Holy Spirit, . . . will teach you everything, and remind you of all that I have said to you" (John 14:25). When we evangelize, the Holy Spirit works through us, continuing the saving work of Jesus. We are helped by the Holy Spirit, as we plant and nourish the seed of faith through our words and actions. Our efforts, moved by the Holy Spirit, enable God to give the increase. Completing the agenda of evangelization is up to God, not us.

9. Process-Oriented

Conversion is a lifelong process. During various stages of our lives, we change, we face new pressures and tensions, and we develop new relationships and opportunities. Each of these changes brings new challenges. During the changes involved with living, we are faced with the deeper mystery of our purpose and destiny.

When looking at the new evangelization in light of the life changes that every person experiences, we *can* realize more fully that evangelization lasts a lifetime. Hence, in considering the new evangelization, we come to see that it includes ongoing efforts to discover the mystery of God's kingdom on earth, as we journey through life to the final realization of God's kingdom in heaven.

On this journey, life constantly challenges us to intensify and deepen our faith, as well as to reach out to the needy and poor, and to serve them as Jesus did while on earth. To reach our final destiny in heaven, the Catholic Church emphasizes that both faith and good works are necessary for salvation.

10. Constant and Consistent in Orientation

The message proclaimed by Catholic evangelization remains constant through the ages. It centers on Jesus' teachings, as interpreted

141

within the living Catholic Tradition. Its teaching is consistent. While shifting emphasis to meet different cultural and historical challenges, its core message is the same. Based in the living Tradition coming down from the apostles, evangelization is always new, because the Holy Spirit continually invites Christians to apply God's Word to a changing world. For this to happen, Catholic evangelization holds firm to the *basics* of the faith, while being open to cultural changes.

Proclaiming God's Word clearly and completely in catechesis is essential to the new evangelization. In this regard, Joseph Cardinal Ratzinger, when addressing the essential contents of the new evangelization, mentioned the following: Conversion, Kingdom, Jesus, and Eternal life (*Address to Catechists and Religion Teachers*, December 12, 2000).

The Catholic pastoral evangelizer helps parish members appreciate the real *fundamentals* of the faith and invites them to use these basic beliefs as stable guides for action. The consistently directive character of Catholic evangelization acknowledges that God's Word and the Eucharist are keys that unlock life's meaning at its deepest level. In this regard, Catholic evangelization provides a stable anchor in an uncertain world.

A Catholic Focus

"Balanced" is a word that summarizes Catholic evangelization. Its balance encompasses family, world, and Church. It extends to the ministries of word, worship, and service. This balance, characterizing Catholic evangelization, begins in God, is enfleshed in Jesus, is carried out through the power of the Holy Spirit, and invites parishioners to holiness and wholeness.

The new evangelization is characterized by *balance*. This balance includes a general orientation that, in theological terms, might be referred to as "every Christian's calling to evangelize from Baptism onward." This responsibility to spread the kingdom of God is not an accessory to faith, but an essential part of living the Gospel. Without such a deep faith conviction on the part of martyrs and confessors, the early Church would never have developed as it did. Whereas today's Christian is often reluctant to share Jesus' message beyond the parish walls, the early followers of Christ eagerly proclaimed his message, even to death.

Another aspect of balance centers on an *interior attitude* that moves the Christian to evangelize as a regular part of one's life orientation. This dimension of living the life of Christ establishes the foundation for all external actions that proclaim the Gospel. If Christians develop this attitude, their response to the needy is like an arrow that hones in on hurting and broken people and reaches out to them as Jesus did. This fundamental interior attitude, moving a Christian to action, is the heart and soul of the Christian evangelizer.

Such an approach to suffering people remains active in my soul after undergoing a painful sickness many years ago. Here is part of the reason why.

I was driving home with my three nieces and nephews on a rainy, slippery night, when a Volkswagen car suddenly skidded into my car from the front. All of us were stunned, and almost immediately I felt a piercing pain in my neck. As a precaution, the police took all of us to the hospital for X-rays. They soon released us, saying there were no serious injuries.

I returned home, but the next day I began to feel my strength ebbing out of me. (All of this happened in the beginning of my second year teaching in the seminary, during the tumultuous years of the late 1960s.) Over the span of a few weeks, I lost much of my strength, and I felt an almost constant pain in my side. When this persisted for a day or so, I was taken again to the hospital, and the doctor diagnosed that I had appendicitis.

The next day, when my blood count returned to normal, the doctor did not operate but sent me home. I did not get better. Slowly, I deteriorated, with no one knowing what was wrong with me or what to do with me. Depression set in. I felt all alone, as though I was trapped in a huge bubble from which I could not emerge. I struggled to teach, but the results were tolerable at best.

Slowly, fall moved into winter and then to spring. I stayed in my room most of the time, with little strength or energy. After months, I wondered why my friends rarely visited me. Eventually, I realized that they did not know how to deal with me in my condition, so they stayed away. In the midst of my physical and emotional pain, my only consolation was the crucifix, hanging on the wall. I'd often beat my head against the plaster wall behind the crucifix and cried out, "Why? Why me? Why did you have to die on the cross?" In time, I better appreciated why Jesus died for me and for other hurting people. Buoyed up with this insight, I could say with some courage, "If you can make it, so can I."

As the months passed, Easter and summertime arrived, and I slowly regained my strength. I realized, then, that something far more profound had happened. I knew that I was different, having changed from a highly competitive, strong athlete, primarily concerned with winning and achieving, to a person who now saw in the most vulnerable among us the face of Christ. My heart and soul changed.

Now the primary motivating force that moves me to help others in their brokenness is the desire to reach out to them, as some did to me, when I was sick. Those whom I least expected stood by me. Now I want to do likewise. Such support and prayer for the weak and vulnerable is the heart of evangelization. I feel no greater privilege than to be numbered with this group.

I tell my story because I hope readers recognize, as I did, that moments that could lead to despair can also motivate people to never give up and eventually to share Jesus' compassion and love, as the new evangelization calls us to do. Such motivation and the actions flowing from it are the groundwork of parish efforts to develop new methods to evangelize. In our brokenness, we look ultimately to the cross for strength, for the new evangelization is about a person, the Son of God, Jesus Christ. All evangelizing efforts swirl around him, as the earth goes around the sun.

II. The New Evangelization — Catholic Style: Pastoral Reflections and Action Steps

The uniqueness of the Catholic approach to evangelization offers many challenges and points of reflection. This section offers certain pastoral reflections and action steps.

Pastoral Reflections

a. What do you think makes the new evangelization distinctively Catholic?

b. Which of the ten characteristics of the new evangelization does your parish do well? Which of them does the parish need to strengthen or improve?

c. In what ways can we say that the new evangelization is balanced?

Action Steps

    a. Arrange a series of parish discussions on the ten characteristics of Catholic evangelization, probing with the parishioners how the parish can integrate them more effectively into its life and ministry.

    b. Set up a parish retreat to consider the ten characteristics of Catholic evangelization.

Chapter Eleven

The New Evangelization and Pastoral Life: A Practical Process

The new evangelization challenges parishes to search for more effective ways to evangelize. This chapter presents a practical process for developing parish evangelization. It is divided into three sections. Section one presents practical ways for a parish to proceed, including segments on personalistic leadership, a modified approach, as well as the new media and the new evangelization. Pitfalls to avoid is the subject of section two. Section three offers suggestions for pastoral reflections and action steps.

---

1. Practical Ways for a Parish to Proceed

A goal of every parish is to help parishioners realize their part in the new evangelization. This includes outreach to Church members, alienated Catholics, and unchurched people. Any pastoral plan for evangelization implies two dynamics: spiritual renewal and shared faith.

Because parishes differ in size, location, leadership, ethnic mix, parishioner mobility, and needs, evangelization models will differ according to local circumstances. At the same time, some suggestions can help parishes develop effective evangelization. This section considers where to begin, how to proceed, with segments on personalistic leadership, a modified approach, as well as the new media and the new evangelization.

Where to Begin

Thy Kingdom Come (p. 9) offers valuable insights into the centrality of parish evangelization. We read,

147

Since evangelization is the essential mission of the Church and parish is the Church present in a given place, all parishes should have evangelization teams, or at least individual evangelizers, working closely with the pastor, council, and staff. An evangelization team is not a luxury or an addition, but a part of normal parish planning, normal parish life. Making this fundamental point to the pastor and parish leadership is perhaps the most important act of evangelization diocesan designates perform. The long-term effectiveness of their ministry depends on how successfully they can move evangelization from the "take-it-or-leave-it" margin to the "must-do" core.

The new evangelization begins by looking to Jesus for guidance. He began his public ministry by calling a few disciples and teaching them his message. Following in Jesus' footsteps, parish evangelization often begins with someone taking a leadership role and inviting several parishioners to join an evangelization effort. The initiative for the new evangelization may begin with the pastor, but it can come from a pastoral leader or parishioner who begins an evangelization effort with his approval. Without the pastor's blessing, parish evangelization has limited success. The following steps suggest a way for parish leaders to begin:

1. *Designate* a parish evangelization coordinator. This person can be someone already interested in and knowledgeable about evangelization, or a person enthusiastic and capable of learning about evangelization and coordinating small groups.

2. *Identify* parishioners willing to look into the meaning of the new evangelization in personal and parish life. The parishioners selected, usually four to seven, become the *evangelization team* or something similar. This team does not do all the one-on-one evangelization in the parish, but discerns ways that the parish as a whole can effectively evangelize. The team exercises an overseeing role. It is not responsible for all parish evangelization. The evangelization team can serve as a dynamic group leading the entire parish to evangelize.

   Referring to the selection on evangelization team members, *Thy Kingdom Come* states, "The pastor should take a very active role in this discernment, since he will be working very closely with parish team members as they carry out their mission." Then, it continues, "In general, the parish evangelization team will include active Catholics with a real enthusiasm for their faith and the ability to draw people into the love of Jesus and the Catholic way of life" (pp. 9-10).

3. *Decide* the most effective way for an evangelization team to begin. Preparation for its ministry includes prayer and discernment. *Thy Kingdom Come* reiterates the importance of team preparation, saying, "Formation should involve prayer, spirituality, in-depth Scripture study, practice in community-building, an analysis of the state of the local church, and an overview of Catholic teaching, including church history" (p. 10).

A big temptation to avoid for a newly formed evangelization team is the need to produce immediate results. This can be a big pitfall, especially if the team has a number of "result-oriented" people on it. The team cannot succumb to this heresy in action, but must take time to ascertain how the Holy Spirit invites this particular parish to evangelize. Several suggestions help facilitate this process:

- Begin with a day of prayer or retreat.
- Center weekly group meetings on prayer, Scripture, and Church teachings about evangelization. The agenda of team meetings can include studying the Christian Scriptures and reflecting on how Jesus and his disciples evangelized, learning various dimensions of Catholic evangelization, and reading Church instructions on evangelization, especially Pope Paul VI's *On Evangelization in the Modern World*. Without a solid biblical base, the evangelization team can get sidetracked by the numbers game, competition, or exclusivity. Without a grounding in Church documents, the evangelization team may miss its link with the larger ecclesial community. The evangelization team needs to spend time, maybe as much as several months, preparing for its ministry through prayer, study, and reflection.
- As the team comes to appreciate Jesus' evangelizing message, it asks, "How can this message best be applied in our parish? What are the parishioners' needs?"
- When the team identifies its focus, the pastor's role becomes more important. If he is not a member of the team, he is invited to join, for the pastor is the chief parish evangelizer. If he chooses not to join the team, he is kept informed about what is happening.

How to Proceed

No single model exists to establish an effective parish evangelization process, but certain points are clear:

1. An effective evangelization process requires the pastor's cooperation and leadership. This first step is critical. The pastor's personal support, liturgical ministry of preaching, catechetical responsibilities, and administrative decisions on hiring personnel and allocating parish funds affect the success of parish evangelization.

2. The next step is for the pastor to approach various parish leaders and invite them to make a commitment to evangelization. These leaders include the school principal, religious-education director, parish council president, finance committee chairperson, St. Vincent de Paul coordinator, liturgical director, and youth minister. These people need to understand their role in raising the awareness of the parish to its evangelical responsibilities. Only after parish leaders acknowledge the parish's responsibility to evangelize is it possible to transform the parish into an evangelizing parish.

   As this occurs, a parish needs to hire future staff leaders committed to evangelization in their specific ministries. Likewise, parish members must accept the parish's call to evangelize if they are to serve in parish leadership roles, such as the education commission, pastoral council, athletic board, and finance council. The latter must be convinced of the parish's commitment to evangelization. Otherwise, monies can easily be spent on misplaced parish priorities.

   Generally, an evangelizing parish does not need new committees or organizational structures. In an evangelizing parish, people in existing organizations accept their responsibility to evangelize the parish community in their role of proclaiming Jesus' Good News.

3. The final step involves actual outreach by parish leaders to the broader parish. As this happens, the evangelization team supports and advises various parish committees and leaders, who, in turn, evangelize parishioners. Several recommendations may help:

- The pastoral team, including the pastor and parish staff, formulates a practical parish evangelization plan. Responsibility to develop this plan can be given to the evangelization team, which submits its recommendations to the pastoral team or pastoral council for modification. In this process, the pastor gives the final approval.

- The pastoral evangelization plan takes into account the parish's needs, such as evangelizing youth, reconciling alienated Catholics, and reaching out to unchurched people. In addition, it includes ways that parish leaders and organizations can cooperate in whatever is done. It also suggests ways for parishioners to see their responsibility to evangelize. Finally, it establishes a timetable and an ongoing method of evaluation.

- A mission or spiritual renewal can initiate the wider parish into its role in evangelization.

- Every parish leader is to communicate the parish evangelization plan to his or her organization. The cooperation of pastoral council members, schoolteachers, catechists, choir members, servers, ushers, coaches, and so on is necessary. This commitment to evangelization is ongoing, as parish personnel change. The pastor reiterates the parish's evangelization commitment in homilies, and he encourages parishioners to extend hospitality to all in the liturgy, meetings, parish socials, and rectory.

- As the new evangelization becomes known to parishioners through homilies, announcements, encouragement of parish leaders, youth groups, and parish organizations, the parish provides opportunities for parishioners to learn more about Scripture, Church teaching, and prayer. This can help parishioners see themselves as evangelizers in their homes, with friends, among alienated Catholics, with the unchurched, in their neighborhoods, and with the civic community. A feedback system is set up between parishioners and parish leaders to reach needy people and to contact potential new parish members.

- As the evangelization movement builds, the evangelization team responds by preparing new evangelizers. *Thy Kingdom*

Come speaks of training evangelists for ministries "like home visitation, or at least directing them to training opportunities" (p. 11). The new evangelization provides opportunities for parishioners to get the necessary skills to do so.

Personalistic Leadership

A parish requires strong leadership from the pastor and staff to most effectively realize its goal of becoming an evangelizing parish. This was illustrated in St. Athanasius Parish.

For years, parishioners tried different ways to evangelize. They set up various evangelization team models, sent out postcards, used other means of advertising to everyone in the geographical confines of the parish, and had meeting after meeting. The results were minimal.

After Father Smith, the new pastor, came to the parish, he began by arranging group meetings of parishioners in their homes so that he could meet them and listen to their concerns. This took the better part of the year.

Father Smith was always seen before and after the Sunday Masses, introducing himself to every visitor. He attended parish meetings, visited the sick, and made himself available to parishioners when they needed him. In time, he hired a staff committed to this same, personalistic approach, whether in the rectory, the school, on the athletic field, in the liturgy, or in the parish school of religion. Father Smith preached hospitality from the pulpit, and he taught the parishioners that evangelization is the task of every Christian and of the parish as a whole. Following his lead, the parish devised goals consistent with its mission and developed an effective organizational model.

It took three or four years, but gradually the parishioners began greeting visitors, grew in sensitivity for parish members, and volunteered for various parish events. Through Father Smith's personal, yet consistent leadership, the newly found spirit of St. Athanasius Parish entered every aspect of parish life. The evangelization team continued, but it was largely committed to praying for the success of the broader parish and making suggestions to the pastoral council and parish leaders.

From parishes like this, we learn that the new evangelization is not primarily about developing new programs, but about a new attitude and way of ministering to parishioners, neighbors, and visitors alike.

A Modified Approach

The approach described above is rooted in strong pastoral leadership and in the insights contained in *Thy Kingdom Come*. It presumes that the pastors and parish leaders involved in parish ministry have a strong interest in evangelization. To be effective, they must first survey the scene in their parishes and decide the best approach to take.

In some parishes, other priorities exist, and it may be difficult to focus on evangelization. This may happen for a variety of reasons, including the fact that many pastors have three or more parishes at the same time and can barely keep their heads above water. With such a workload, it is hard enough for a pastor to fulfill his day-to-day responsibilities.

Saying this, however, does not excuse a pastor from acknowledging the vital role of evangelization in parish ministry. It may mean, nonetheless, that not everything outlined above will be practical. In such instances, it is important for other pastoral leaders to secure the pastor's support for any evangelization efforts that they pursue. Without his support, the outlook for effective parish implementation of the new evangelization is not very bright.

Presuming, however, the pastor's indirect cooperation, pastoral leaders can evangelize the ministries for which they are entrusted and encourage other segments of the parish to do the same. They can address the new evangelization by encouraging parishioners to take a personalistic approach in greeting visitors at church, sporting events, or the rectory. They can go online and make use of the multiple websites that contain materials on the new evangelization. In particular, youth leaders can challenge young people to take seriously the call of Christ to reach out to their peers, unafraid to share Jesus' Good News with them.

Where the situation of blended parishes exists or several parishes or missions share the same pastor, they must often expend considerable energy in integrating their ministries. Where this is the case, parish leaders can focus on the new evangelization as the prime unifying force of all Church ministries in and beyond the parish.

This was the case in a missionary area where I helped facilitate the coming together of four rural parishes under one pastor. It soon became clear that the prime requirement for success in this endeavor was to overcome doubts and past competition between these parishes at various locations.

A great start was made, not with a lecture or formal meeting, but with a daylong party and celebration, topped off by a huge potluck dinner, with entertainment from local musicians. Banjo and guitar players connected the various parish members in a way that no formal meeting could ever have done.

After that day, more explicit evangelization within the parishes and beyond them forged the bond that enabled the work of God to be effectively proclaimed in the region and to the wider Church. The professional resources to do this were minimal, but because of the leadership of the new pastor and a few parishioners, effective evangelization happened, and the parishes came together. From this, I learned that the prime focus enabling the new evangelization to succeed is the personal witness of faithful Christians. When this happens, it's easier to proclaim Jesus' Good News.

Every place is different, and when an ideal or more formal process seems impossible or difficult to accomplish, interested parish leaders are challenged to adapt the ideal norms described above to the locality where the new evangelization is to be implemented.

The New Media and the New Evangelization

A parish process for the new evangelization must take advantage of the opportunities for communication provided by the new media. Pope Benedict XVI himself took the lead in encouraging the Church to use the new technologies to draw people to Christ and the Church. In his message to the 44th World Communications Day (May 16, 2010), the pope said,

> Responding adequately to this challenge amid today's cultural shifts, to which young people are especially sensitive, necessarily involves using new communications technologies. The world of digital communication, with its almost limitless expressive capacity, makes us appreciate all the more Saint Paul's exclamation: "Woe to me if I do not preach the Gospel" (1 Cor 9:16). The increased availability of the new technologies demands greater responsibility on the part of those called to proclaim the Word, but it also requires them to become more focused, efficient and compelling in their efforts. Priests stand at the threshold of a new era: as new technologies create deeper forms of relationship across greater distances, they

are called to respond pastorally by putting the media ever more effectively at the service of the Word.

A detailed practical introduction to building new media into parish evangelization plans is beyond the scope of this book. But pastoral leaders can include the following in their planning:

1. Develop an attractive and multifaceted website that introduces newcomers to the parish. This can include essential parish information, Mass and confession times, Sunday homilies, pictures of parishioners at parish events, testimonies, basic instruction in Catholic doctrine, and so on.

2. Make wise use of the social media. For example, create a parish page on Facebook, one that allows comments, which can lead to evangelistic opportunities.

3. Use new-media technology for communication with parishioners. Install an efficient e-mail system. And consider using a service such as Flocknote (www.flocknote.com) to coordinate all parish communications.

For a comprehensive way to introduce your parish to the digital revolution, consult Brandon Vogt's *The Church and New Media* and refer to Matt Warner's chapter, "High-Tech Community: New Media in the Parish."

2. Pitfalls to Avoid

First and foremost, parishes should avoid the pitfall of presenting evangelization as a new program. The new evangelization is what Christian life is about — namely, witness, concern, and love. With this in mind, the following suggestions are offered:

1. *Avoid clannishness.* Some parishes seem to deteriorate into clannishness. Evangelization teams cannot fall into the trap of thinking they are special. In a sense they are, but only as humble servants of the Word, as all Christians are called to be. If a sense of elitism develops, little cooperation will happen among parishioners.

2. *Be open and ongoing.* Since parish evangelization is a process, not a product, it is open and ongoing. Parishioners change, and leadership changes. As this happens, accommodations need to be made.

3. *Avoid institutionalization.* Parish evangelization cannot be viewed as a separate ministry. It is *central* to *all* ministry. Among other things, this means that a separate evangelization budget may not always need to be set up. Monies allocated for evangelization can be directed through already-existing parish organizations. For example, the appropriate catechetical, liturgical, service, and youth ministers budget monies for Bibles, books, tapes, and funds for the poor.

4. *Do not base evangelization on money.* Evangelization's success rests on people, not money. A parish leader once said, "We can't do much evangelization because we are a poor parish with little money." Seen from a biblical perspective, another reply is forthcoming: We are limited creatures, and God's Spirit evangelizes through our strengths and brokenness. We do not need expensive programs, special speakers, and media ads to share who we are as followers of Christ. While these may serve the overall evangelization effort, they cannot be the heart of it.

5. *Do not over-structure.* To accomplish their evangelical mission, parish leaders must identify people's needs, organize renewal efforts, and reach out to alienated Catholics, or unchurched people. As this happens, room must be left for the spontaneous workings of the Holy Spirit. When too much bureaucracy exists, structures can become more important than evangelization itself.

6. *Revolve leadership.* Every parish has parishioners who have been *in charge* of this or that task for years or who are over committed. Such loyal parishioners may work in the rectory, coordinate parish functions, direct the choir, or run the St. Vincent de Paul Society. Their loyalty is commendable, but such faithfulness cannot serve as the pretext for discouraging other parish leaders from assuming parish leadership positions or for refusing to turn over responsibilities to them.

The new evangelization may work well with a revolving leadership process for the evangelization team. This can be accomplished through a limited commitment, possibly three years. During the first year, person A is in charge, with person B learning the job as an apprentice. In the second year, person B takes over the leadership, and person C becomes the apprentice, while person A acts as an ad-hoc consultant to person B. In the third year, person B acts as a consultant to person C, who is in charge. Then someone new is brought on board. This continuing process ensures continuity and fresh leadership.

The objective of all parish evangelization is to form Christians who acknowledge their vocation to share their faith. Evangelizers help the broader parish community see this calling. A parish reinvigorates its ministries through evangelization, which invites parishioners to acknowledge their concern for friends, enemies, and all people.

Let our lives reflect the words of *Thy Kingdom Come* (p. 12, quoted from *On Evangelization in the Modern World*), as we accept our baptismal call to evangelize:

> "Having been sent and evangelized, the Church herself sends out evangelizers. She puts on their lips the saving Word, she explains to them the message of which she herself is the depositary, she gives them the mandate which she herself has received and sends them out to preach. . . . There is thus a profound link between Christ, the Church and evangelization. During the period of the Church that we are living in, it is she who has the task of evangelizing. This mandate is not accomplished without her, and still less against her." (EMW, nos. 15-16)

Only in collaboration with the mission of Jesus and the Church do we evangelize most fully. This is our call as disciples of Jesus Christ.

3. The New Evangelization and Pastoral Life: Pastoral Reflections and Action Steps

The new evangelization involves more than fresh insights on how to evangelize. It requires action, as Christian disciples take up their call to evangelize. Parish leaders are challenged to take the lead in this effort.

To help in this work, the following pastoral reflections and action steps are suggested.

Pastoral Reflections

- What is the state of evangelization in your parish? What can you do as a pastoral leader to help implement the new evangelization in your parish?

Action Steps

- With the support of the pastor, the pastoral staff can assess the status of evangelization in the parish and the needs of the community. Then they can set aside a substantial period of time to develop a comprehensive plan to implement the new evangelization in the parish.

Conclusion

The new evangelization invites all pastoral leaders to be intentional in their commitment to the new evangelization and to take pride in developing an evangelizing parish. This is a challenging task, but following the suggestions of Pope Benedict XVI, it can start like a small mustard seed and develop slowly. Slow growth, solidly rooted in the rich ground of Scripture and Church teaching, will bear fruit.

This does not happen overnight. It begins with a loving community that welcomes those who want to learn and celebrate Jesus' Good News. This kind of community reaches out to others in a faith-filled and generous way. Such an attitude allows active and inactive Catholics, as well as nonbelievers, to discover the mystery of God's kingdom, as they journey through life.

The new evangelization challenges parishes to look at their spirit, style, and structures, asking whether they connect with parishioners' needs. Regardless of the conclusions reached, every parish needs solid catechesis, good liturgies, and various service activities.

For the new evangelization to grow and mature, parish leaders must get out from behind their desks and into the neighborhoods to connect with the poor and to express compassion for the sick and dying. Finally, it means making alienated Catholics their special concern by listening to them, inviting them back, and welcoming them.

The new evangelization invites Catholic leaders to dream big dreams and to be more nurturing and available, as they help parishioners and visitors appreciate the beauty of Jesus' Good News. This dream remains an eternal hope that motivates pastoral ministers to constantly remember and fulfill their invitation to evangelize.

In this way, new life will be born and the future will be filled with hope. The new evangelization will happen, as said in *Called and Gifted for the Third Millennium*, "if ordained and lay members of Christ's faithful understand their roles and ministries as complementary, and their purposes joined to the one mission and ministry of Jesus Christ" (p. 18).

The new evangelization invites saints and sinners to join hands, ask for the Holy Spirit's *wisdom*, and walk together into the kingdom of God.